Help
a Thief!

Help
a Thief!

... and Other Misadventures
in Punctuation

CAROLINE TAGGART

Michael O'Mara Books Limited

This paperback edition first published in 2021.
First published in Great Britain in 2017 under the title
The Accidental Apostrophe
by Michael O'Mara Books Limited
9 Lion Yard
Tremadoc Road
London SW4 7NQ

A CIP catalogue record for this book is available from the British Library.

Papers used by Michael O'Mara Books Limited are natural, recyclable products made from wood grown in sustainable forests. The manufacturing processes conform to the environmental regulations of the country of origin.

ISBN: 978-1-78929-361-6 in paperback print format
ISBN: 978-1-78243-821-2 in ebook format

1 2 3 4 5 6 7 8 9 10

www.mombooks.com

Cover Illustration by Jim Benton
Cover design by Natasha Le Coultre
Designed and typeset by Jade Wheaton

Printed and bound by CPI Group (UK) Ltd, Croydon, CR0 4YY

MIX
Paper from
responsible sources
FSC® C020471

*For Rebecca, who somehow
makes it all happen.*

Also by This Author

Contents

Author's note

In the course of this book I have quoted a number of authors and drawn attention to their punctuation. I'm well aware that publishers have individual 'house styles' that impose conventions on their authors; that copy-editors and proofreaders may alter an author's use of commas or hyphens; and that any of these individuals could make a mistake, be inconsistent or just not notice something that perhaps they should have noticed. So when I say, 'This author does ... [whatever it is they do]', I realize that it could be publisher, editor or – in at least two cases – translator who is responsible for the punctuation of the final printed text. I apologize, therefore, if I have singled out the wrong person for criticism or praise.

Introduction

In ancient times, blocks of text were commonly written *justasblockswithoutevenwordspacingnevermindpunctua tion tohelpthereadertointerpretthem. therewasnodistinc tionbetweencapitalsandlowercaseletterseither.* Orators using such texts as notes for a speech would prepare carefully so that they were familiar with the content and didn't come a cropper over a confusion between, say, *The Notable Furniture Company* and *The No Table Furniture Company*. Or the Greek or Latin equivalent.

It was a Greek librarian called Aristophanes (not the playwright), working in the great library of Alexandria in the third century BC, who introduced dots between phrases, to help the reader know where to pause. These were the forerunners of our commas, colons and full stops, but they didn't take the ancient world by storm. With the emphasis still on oratory and on reading aloud, rather than sitting at home quietly with a book, too few people had to bother about them for them to become 'standard usage'.

As we entered the Christian era, sacred texts were widely read (by priests and even sometimes by the rest of us); it became ever more important to remove any likelihood of misinterpretation. To a potential murderer or adulterer, for example, there is a world of difference between 'If you are tempted, yield not, resisting the urge to commit a sin' and 'If you are tempted, yield, not resisting the urge to commit a sin'. And the only thing that has changed is the position of a comma.

But although people recognized that the *idea* of punctuation was important, it took them a while to devise a system. St Augustine of Hippo, writing at the end of the fourth century AD, advised scribes that – if all else failed in the avoidance of ambiguity – 'there is nothing to hinder us to point the sentence according to any method we choose'.

Therein lies the crux of the problem. 'Any method we choose'? What use is that? We need help, not permission to throw punctuation marks about willy-nilly (or should that be willy nilly?). Do we use a dash or a colon? A full stop or a semicolon? Inverted commas or italics? And where does that **** apostrophe go? Come on, Augustine, help us out here.

Aristophanes had been looking at one aspect of punctuation – the symbols themselves – whereas Augustine was talking about quite another – how to use them. As far as the symbols were concerned, from about the seventh to the ninth century, lots of scholars put forward suggestions. St Isidore of Seville deserves an honourable mention, as does Alcuin of York, intellectual mover and shaker at the court of the Holy Roman Emperor Charlemagne. After that, things began to settle down, although illustrated medieval manuscripts allowed their scribes individual variations, touches of personal taste and whimsy. Then, with the invention of the printing press in the fifteenth century, those variations disappeared under a hail of standardization and hot-metal type. To a large extent, the marks that Gutenberg was using in the 1450s reached the twenty-first century unscathed and un-improved upon.

Hold that thought: we'll be coming back to it later in the book.

So much for the symbols; what about the system that explained how to use them? Well, many centuries on from St Augustine, there were still surprisingly few hard and fast rules. Here's what an anonymous *Short Introduction to English Grammar* said in 1791:

> *. . . the doctrine of Punctuation must needs be very imperfect: few precise rules can be given which will hold without exception in all cases; but much must be left to the judgment and taste of the writer.*

On the other hand, if a greater number of marks were invented to express all the possible different pauses of pronunciation, the doctrine of them would be very perplexed and difficult, and the use of them would rather embarrass than assist the reader.

It remains, therefore, that we be content with the Rules of Punctuation, laid down with as much exactness as the nature of the subject will admit: such as may serve for a general direction, to be accommodated to different occasions; and to be supplied, where sufficient, by the writer's judgment.

Even today, many experts admit that quite a lot of punctuation is down to taste, or to your own or a publisher's established style. Just as some publishers insist on spellings such as *organization* and *realize*, while others require *organisation* and *realise*, so some will use a serial comma (see page 39) and have a view on whether or not to hyphenate *postmodernism*. You may, of course, have your own opinions and want to act on them.

So what this book aims to do is to clarify the rules that do exist, because - to introduce a handy example of dashes - you may never have learned them, or may have learned them a while ago [time to drop in a semicolon]; it also sets out the options where the choice is yours. In addition, it will express a view on what does and doesn't matter, what you can get away with and what simply won't do. And, whenever it can, it will introduce examples to show that, contrary to what many people believe [and throwing in a pair of bracketing commas], punctuation is [here is a colon introducing a list]:

- not that difficult really
- important in making your meaning clear.

Ready? Then take a deep breath and let's [that's an apostrophe indicating that a letter has been left out] get started.

1

Things the Experts Do

To begin with a comforting thought: if you want to ignore the rules, you'll be in good company.

A lot of punctuation is about convention. The conventional way to break up a long piece of text, for example - once you've got used to the idea of putting spaces between the words - is to start a new paragraph. Most writers do this every time they change the subject, change the mood, change the setting, move forwards or backwards in time. There are no hard and fast rules about how long a paragraph needs to be: it can be a full page, creating an atmosphere or developing a thought; or just a few lines, short and choppy to convey movement and excitement. One reason for paragraphing is that trying to decipher huge blocks of text can be offputting. Many readers will be intimidated by the lack of white space on a page that dividing text into manageable chunks gives.

With dialogue (in a novel rather than in a play or script, which have their own rules), each new speaker generally has a new paragraph. That's because it is easy for a reader to get lost when more than one character is speaking. Conventional British punctuation gives the additional assistance of putting quotation marks round the actual words spoken. Other nationalities use different devices, but again they do it when they are using *conventional* punctuation.

The Portuguese writer José Saramago broke these rules completely in his novel *Blindness*. Most of his paragraphs are two pages long and there are no new paragraphs for dialogue. I don't know why he chose to do that, but it was his eighteenth novel and he was three years away from winning the Nobel Prize. I suggest that when you're at that stage of your writing career, you can take the law into your own hands too. Perhaps not much before that, though.

It isn't just the Portuguese. The Australian Murray Bail, in his novel *The Voyage*, has a number of paragraphs that last more than ten pages (admittedly in quite generously spaced type) and, although he uses conventional 'speech marks', he frequently has several characters' dialogue run together in the same paragraph.

In *Ulysses*, James Joyce chooses to omit the apostrophes

in words such as *I'll*, *I've* and *I'd* and he isn't hot on hyphens: in the course of the book he writes *knockkneed*, *allimportant* and *willowpatterned* as one word, as well as creations of his own such as *bullockbefriending* and *gigglegold*. Perhaps weirdest of all (though there is a lot of competition for that title) are *halffed*, which surely cries out for a hyphen between the two *f*s, and *hangerson*, which at a glance looks as if it could be divided as *hanger-son*, meaning the offspring of an executioner. Or perhaps as *han-gerson*, somehow rhyming with *person* and meaning goodness knows what.

If you can't bring yourself to care about hyphens, Molly Bloom's famous interior monologue, which ends *Ulysses*, runs in my Penguin edition to sixty-three pages divided into a mere eight paragraphs, with one full stop (at the very end) and no commas at all. You *really* can't afford to let your mind wander. It's noticeable, however, that in dramatizations of the monologue (and don't take my word for it: there are plenty of them on YouTube), the actor hesitates, often at some length, as she ponders her own thoughts; she puts in the pauses that might have been indicated on the page by commas, full stops and ellipses or dashes; she uses a normal rising intonation for a question. You couldn't speak it otherwise – it would make no sense, and after a while you wouldn't be able to breathe.

Ten years or so after *Ulysses*, Gertrude Stein – another author not renowned for her concessions to the inattentive reader – was producing sentences like this:

There were printed of this edition I forget whether it was seven hundred and fifty or a thousand copies but at any rate it was a very charming little book and Gertrude Stein was enormously pleased, and it, as every one knows, had an enormous influence on all young writers and started off columnists in the newspapers of the whole country on their long campaign of ridicule.

A conscientious copy-editor might have suggested introducing at least one more comma, one more full stop and perhaps a couple of dashes, in an effort both to promote clarity and to avoid the threatened ridicule. (At this point, my own conscientious editor asked if I had got this right: was Gertrude Stein really writing about herself in the third person? I started to explain about *The Autobiography of Alice B. Toklas*, which is by Gertrude Stein and therefore isn't the autobiography of Alice B. Toklas at all, although it's written as if it were. Then we agreed (1) that life was too short and (2) that it all added to Gertrude Stein's incomprehensibility, which sort of confirmed what I was trying to say but was drifting us quite a long way from the subject of punctuation.)

Then, in the 1960s, along came Hubert Selby Jr with *Last Exit to Brooklyn*, chunks of which are written in a sort of Brooklyn patois, not bothering with quotation marks for dialogue or with apostrophes, and using idiosyncratic spelling such as *whereya gonna go* and *the next thing yaknow the lawll be knockin on my door*. And in the 1990s

James Kelman won the Booker Prize with *How Late It Was, How Late*, which also eschews quotation marks and sometimes ends a paragraph without a full stop and begins a new one without a capital letter. More recently, Will Self's *Shark*, published in 2014, begins (without a capital letter) in the middle of a sentence and is written as one 466-page paragraph – no chapter breaks and again no quotation marks. But it makes copious use of italics, dashes and ellipses, which may or may not be intended to be helpful to the reader.

Ulysses and *Last Exit* have both been banned at some point in their careers, while *How Late It Was* attracted adverse comment for its copious use of the F word. Yet D. H. Lawrence managed to work a semicolon and the notorious C word into the same paragraph of *Lady Chatterley's Lover*, so it clearly isn't essential to ignore punctuation in order to write explicitly about sex.

The point I am trying to make – and will make intermittently throughout this book – is that these authors deliberately adopted an unconventional style. They did it for reasons of their own, and it is entirely their privilege. Many people maintain that *Ulysses* is the greatest novel of the twentieth century; *Last Exit* is a cult classic that has been praised for its frank depiction of previously taboo subjects such as homosexuality and domestic violence; Gertrude Stein was undeniably right when she wrote that a rose is a rose is a rose. But none of these writers made their works any easier to read by messing about with punctuation; indeed,

Joyce threw those sixty-three stream-of-consciousness pages at readers who had already ploughed through over eight hundred to get there and might have felt they deserved an easier run at the finishing line. Okay, the man was a genius, but still . . .

As a creative writer, you may want to emulate Joyce or Selby, Saramago or Bail, or you may decide to go your own way and make up a non-system of your own. But it's easier to break rules and conventions if you know what they are in the first place. And, at the other end of the writing spectrum, if you want people to take a quick look at what you have written on the page or on the screen and be able to understand instantly what you mean, you may find some of what follows useful.

~

2

Things That Clarify: I

A sentence may be defined as *a sequence of words capable of standing alone to make an assertion, ask a question or give a command*. So let's start by considering how sentences begin and end.

Full stops

> **Full stop (.)**: *the punctuation mark used at the end of a sentence that is neither a question nor an exclamation; also used after some abbreviations.*

A *full stop* is also called a *point* or *full point*; in North America it is a *period*. All these terms mean the same thing. I use *full stop* because it's what I learned at school, not because it is better or worse than any of the others.

As the definition above explains, a full stop comes at the end of a sentence. This can be a simple, one-clause sentence:

I went to bed early.

He handed in his notice.

They should be here soon.

Or it can be more complex:

I went to bed early: I had had several late nights in a row and there was nothing on television.

He handed in his notice after his boss had yelled at him in front of the entire office – he wasn't going to put up with that sort of thing.

They should be here soon, assuming that they left on time and they don't get caught up in traffic.

As in these longer examples, there may be other pieces of punctuation along the way but, unless the sentence requires a question mark or an exclamation mark, what comes at the end is a full stop, and it is followed by a capital letter, marking the beginning of the next sentence.

Straightforward enough at first glance. But on closer examination, not as straightforward as all that.

Because if you look at the previous paragraph, you'll see that the full stops come at the end not of complete sentences but of what are called *sentence fragments* – bits of sentences, lacking a finite verb, that we can make sense of because of what has gone before. *Straightforward enough at first glance* doesn't have the vestige of a verb in it; nor does *But on closer examination, not as straightforward as all that.* If you read them in isolation they wouldn't tell you much. But in context they do. In your mind you can expand them to mean *that definition* seems [finite verb] *straightforward enough at first glance. But on closer examination, it* is [finite verb] *not as straightforward as all that.*

Another example: *Breakfast was magnificent. Eggs any style. Bacon from the local farm. Mushrooms from the local fields. And, most importantly, an apparently infinite quantity of tea.*

Breakfast was magnificent is a sentence, *was* being the finite verb. But all the rest are fragments, with the words *there were* or *there was* understood. But they still begin with a capital letter, have a full stop at the end and are followed by another capital.

See also the use of full stops in abbreviations and contractions, page 152.

Capital letters

> **Capital:** *the large letter used at the beginning of a sentence or to denote a proper name; also often used in abbreviations and acronyms.*

In his novel *Golden Hill*, Francis Spufford has his hero write a letter to his father, which begins:

You have warned me so many Times, of the Dangers of the World, for such as Us, should We but stray one Step beyond the Bounds of our Safety ...

That looks very odd to the modern eye, but the book, although published in 2016, is set in 1746, when capital letters were used much more than they are today. Twenty-first-century style tends to keep them to a minimum: it would have begun the sentence with a capital *Y* and left it at that.

That said, capitals are compulsory for:

- the first word of a sentence or of a line of poetry
- the pronoun *I*, whether it is at the beginning of a sentence or not
- names of people, places and buildings: *George, Meera, Mrs Jones, Toronto, the Mississippi, Fleet Street, Sydney Opera House*
- other proper nouns, such as the names of companies and institutions: *Toyota, Burger King, the Pentagon*; and nicknames: *the People's Princess, the Big Apple*
- adjectives derived from proper nouns: *the German people, the Amazonian rainforest, Georgian architecture, Shakespearean sonnets*

- the principal words (see box, below) in the title of a book, play, film, work of art, piece of music, etc.: *Game of Thrones, Romeo and Juliet, 12 Years a Slave, The Birth of Venus, Rhapsody in Blue*

What's a principal word?

To expand on the point about principal words (see main text) it's probably easier to identify the minor words – the ones that *shouldn't* be capitalized. These are generally:

- articles (*a, an, the*), unless they are the first word of the title
- co-ordinating conjunctions such as *and, but, or, nor.*
- short prepositions such as *to, at, on, in.* Capitalize any that are four letters or more, such as *over, under, behind, along, through.* (Many pundits say five letters or more, but most versions of *One Flew Over the Cuckoo's Nest* break this rule, so I'm going for four.)

Capitalize everything else and you won't go far wrong. But note that if you ask Word to 'change case' to Title Case, it will capitalize the first letter of every word and you will need to change back *and, the* and what-have-you to lower case.

- days of the week, months of the year and festival days such as *Easter, Eid, Hanukkah* and *Diwali*

- titles that precede people's names: *Dr Watson, Reverend Green, Colonel Mustard, Miss Scarlett*
- abbreviations and acronyms: *BBC, FBI, UNESCO*
- brand names: *Heinz, Kraft, Smirnoff*

It is not necessary to capitalize the seasons of the year (*spring, summer, autumn, winter*) unless they are part of a title (*The Silent Spring, Autumn in New York*) or a set phrase referring to a specific period: *the Arab Spring, the Winter of Discontent*. Nor should you give the word *century* a capital *c* unless there is good reason to do so: phrases such as *in the fourteenth century, eighteenth-century fashions* or *twentieth-century art* all manage perfectly well without.

New Age and occult writers have a tendency to capitalize words such as *Nature, Spirit* and *Death*, endowing these abstract entities with a personal quality. It's not a million miles from calling an unnamed deity *God*, and it's fine in the right context.

Earth can be tricky: in a sequence that sets it between Venus and Mars, it's a place name and has a capital; in a gardening context, when it means nothing more than *soil*, it doesn't. But what about *when dinosaurs walked the earth*? Does this mean the dinosaurs were on this planet, or that they were walking on soil rather than water or tarmac? I'm inclined to think it's something in between and would go with St Augustine – 'use any method you choose'. Not the decisive answer you were hoping for? Well, to help you make up your mind, consider the style of the rest of your text. If you're capitalizing Nature, capitalize Earth as well.

As for compass points - north, south, east and west and their derivatives - they need capitals *only* when they refer to some specific, recognized geographical or political area: *the American South, the Wild West, East Germany, the Northern Territory (of Australia)*. Or, like the seasons, if they are in titles: *North by Northwest, East of Eden, South Park*. Don't capitalize them in *he drove north for three hours* or *Naples is 200 km southeast of Rome*. You can make subtle distinctions, though: *the west coast of the United States* might mean nothing more than the strip of land lying closest to the Pacific shore; *the West Coast mentality* implies - stereotypically - a laid-back, tolerant attitude to life at variance with the fast-paced, get-up-and-go of the East. You wouldn't write *west coast mentality* in lower case.

The French have a capital for it

Just as the names of countries and cities have capital letters, so do their derived adjectives: *French, Russian, American, Parisian, Muscovite, Angeleno*. There are those who maintain that such words need capitals only when they apply to the nationality - *French literature*, perhaps, or *Russian politics* - but not to something that isn't really French or Russian at all, such as *french dressing* or *russian roulette*. Personally I think spelling these words with a small letter looks very odd, while the argument that you are making a distinction between a dressing made in France and a dressing made to a style that may have

→

originated in France is pernickety in the extreme. How often are you likely to want to differentiate between the particular variation of a certain gambling game that is played in Russia and an act of bravado with a partially loaded gun? I'm guessing not very often at all.

They do and they don't

Question marks arise over words that are sometimes capitalized and sometimes not. *Buckingham Palace*, for example, is clearly a proper name and *palace* should have a capital. *He was invited to collect his award from the Palace* refers specifically to Buckingham Palace and as such is capitalized, too. But in *her country house was more like a palace than anywhere I had ever stayed*, *palace* is a common noun, referring to any old palace, and begins with a small letter.

Similarly:

Over the centuries, the Church has had to change its attitude to divorce (the Church is an institution)

The church in the village dates back to Norman times (the church is merely a building)

The Golden Age of Spanish literature began with Columbus's voyages and ended with the death of the playwright Calderón (a specific period, in this case 1492–1681)

The London 2012 Olympics ushered in a golden age of British sport (not a specific period, merely a remarkably good time)

The word *age* (and similar ones such as *period* and *era*) can cause problems. In most of the sources I've checked, geological time follows the style *Pleistocene epoch*, *Mesozoic era*, *Jurassic period*, though I'd be hard pushed to argue logically against *Pleistocene Epoch* etc. As so often, it's a matter of choosing a style and sticking to it. Or, in the case of geology and palaeontology, getting round the problem by referring simply to *the Pleistocene*, *the Mesozoic* and *the Jurassic*. That's also a boon for those of us who have a soft spot for dinosaurs but don't know our epochs from our eons.

Naming no names

Here's another example of a capital referring to the specific, while a lower-case initial indicates something generic.

I was reading recently about some research conducted by *a London-hospital-based group of scientists*. It occurred to me that there used to be an institution called the London Hospital. It's where John Merrick, the Elephant Man, spent the last years of his life, but that is neither here nor there. The point is that the research I was reading about had presumably not been carried out at the London Hospital; if it had been, the author would have used a capital H or written *a group of scientists based at the London Hospital*. The lower case tells us that she was talking about an unspecified London hospital, one that she was choosing not to name.

~

3

Things That Clarify: II

Comma (,): the punctuation mark indicating a slight pause in a sentence and used to distinguish items in a list or to separate a non-restrictive clause or phrase from a main clause.

The massive success of Lynne Truss's book *Eats, Shoots and Leaves* drew the world's attention to the importance of the comma; since then, the expression *Let's eat Grandma* has been widely used for a similar purpose. The comma in the first example changes the phrase from a summary of a panda's diet to a description of the way a hungry gunslinger might behave in a café. The lack of one after 'eat' in the second turns a request from a hungry grandchild into a macabre piece of incestuous cannibalism.

These are artificial examples, made up to make a point. As was the text message I received from a friend who knew I was writing this book and to whom I had suggested we had tea on Sunday, as we often do. She'd been about to reply 'Well, stranger things have happened' when she realized that adding a second comma would change the entire meaning of the words. 'Well, stranger, things have happened' made no sense in the context, but, as I say, it illustrated a point.

A genuine instance, though, came from another friend, who runs a small bakery. A customer texted to ask if one of her cakes was suitable for vegetarians.

'Well, it has eggs in it, if that's what you mean,' my friend replied.

In response to this came the unpunctuated message, 'No eggs are fine.' The customer – who was vegetarian rather than vegan – had meant to be reassuring but, by failing to put a comma after *no*, had sent a message that meant the exact opposite of what she intended.

So shall we agree that there are times when commas matter? Including when you're making cakes.

Mini-breaks

Although all commas do fundamentally the same thing (create a small break), there are lots of different places where they can do it. So here are some guidelines as to where they go.

- After a word or phrase that precedes and is separate from the main clause:

  In fourteen hundred and ninety-two, Columbus sailed the ocean blue.

  After twenty minutes of holding on and listening to Vivaldi, I finally got through to the call centre.

  Yes, I am free on Tuesday.

  However, I'd prefer to come on Thursday if that suited you.

- Before a word, phrase or clause that comes after and is separate from the main clause:

  I could see you on Thursday, maybe.

  I want to go out, whatever the weather.

  I could finish the job by this evening, if only you would stop interrupting me.

- Before what is known as a 'question tag', in sentences such as:

  You are happy with the arrangements, aren't you?

  We ought to pay their expenses, don't you think?

  He wasn't upset, was he?

- Between clauses within the same sentence:

  If I go to bed late, I have bad dreams, even if I haven't been eating cheese.

In summer, she always got up early, whereas in winter you had to drag her out of bed.

- Before conjunctions such as *although*, *but*, *or*, *so* and *yet* when they link two independent clauses (and see the section on semicolons, page 85, for more about links like this):

  The speaker was entertaining, although he didn't tell us anything we didn't know.

  It's officially springtime, but it still feels very cold.

  I heard a footstep, or perhaps a floorboard creaking.

  I'm going to be late, so please start dinner without me.

  There was a crowd outside the courthouse, yet no one seemed to have heard the verdict.

- Before the word *too* at the end of a sentence when it means *also*; or before and after it to add emphasis in the middle of a sentence:

  I love Venice, but I quite like Florence, too.

  The Smiths, too, were to spend their holidays in Italy.

- Before, or before and after, words such as *though*, *however*, *perhaps*, *eventually* in constructions such as:

  She was happy enough in her job; sometimes, though, she wondered if she ought to show more ambition.

  Your suit is very smart. I suggest, however, that you wear a less garish tie.

You could think about getting a haircut, perhaps.

He knew that, eventually, the police would find out.

How long? Or how many?

Here's another ambiguous statement:

For the last few years at least a hundred thousand migrating birds have appeared each winter.

Does it mean that the birds have been coming for at least the last few years, but possibly longer? (*For the last few years at least, a hundred thousand migrating birds have appeared each winter.*) Or that there are at least a hundred thousand birds, but possibly more? (*For the last few years, at least a hundred thousand migrating birds have appeared each winter.*) A comma would tell us.

• In constructions such as

His shirt was pink, his tie dark red ...

The restaurant was candlelit, the atmosphere romantic ...

... where a conjunction such as *and* or *but* and the verb in the second part of the sentence are understood but not expressed.

• In addresses, and in place names where part of the name gives additional information about the other:

1600 Pennsylvania Avenue, Washington, DC.

The Roald Dahl Museum is in Great Missenden, Buckinghamshire.

The latter example serves the double function of telling you where Great Missenden is if you've never heard of it, and of distinguishing it from the Great Missendens you might have heard of in Yorkshire, Tuscany or Uzbekistan. The same applies to the title of the film *Paris, Texas*, which distinguishes the so-called 'best small town in Texas' from the place that some Americans call Paris, France, and that the rest of us call Paris.

Note that if those sentences continued, you'd need a comma after *DC* and *Buckinghamshire*, too:

1600 Pennsylvania Avenue, Washington, DC, is the address of the White House.

The Roald Dahl Museum is in Great Missenden, Buckinghamshire, and is usually closed on Mondays.

A list to starboard

One of the comma's most common functions is to separate items in a list:

Compulsory subjects include English, maths, IT, a foreign language and a science.

Roosevelt, Stalin and Churchill met at the Yalta Conference in 1945.

St Lucia, the Bahamas and the Yucatan Peninsula all offer excellent beach holidays.

When the individual items are longer, lists can become complicated: in the sentence *St Kitts and Nevis, and the Turks and Caicos Islands are both island groups in the Caribbean*, the comma shows that St Kitts and Nevis are to be grouped together, but are separate from the Turks and Caicos. This gets more convoluted if you want to extend the list: *St Kitts and Nevis, the Turks and Caicos Islands, Antigua and Barbuda and St Vincent and the Grenadines*. There's a strong argument here for a serial comma (see below) after Barbuda; in all but the most formal contexts you might also be tempted to opt for ampersands – *St Kitts & Nevis, the Turks & Caicos Islands, Antigua & Barbuda, and St Vincent & the Grenadines* – to link the island groups. Or to resort to semicolons (see page 85).

The serial comma

In a sentence such as *Roosevelt, Stalin and Churchill met at the Yalta Conference in 1945*, most modern British writers would punctuate as I have done. But Americans – and some Brits – would add a comma after Stalin. This is a *serial comma*, also called an *Oxford* or *Harvard comma* because those two universities traditionally advocate it. Like so much punctuation, it's a matter of taste and style.

It's useful, though, in the Caribbean example given above, or in other lists where one or more items consist of more than one word: *the puddings were chocolate mousse, raspberries and cream, and apple pie* makes it clear that the cream comes with the raspberries but not the apple pie. What isn't clear, however, is whether *raspberries and cream* make one dish and *chocolate mousse* another, or whether all three come together. Try reordering – the words, that is, not the puddings – and you come up with an unambiguous choice between *chocolate mousse, apple pie, and raspberries and cream*.

Items in a list can be more than just words and short phrases. Commas are also appropriate in examples such as:

> *Liz wants to go to Durham, Margot to Cambridge, and Sara has her sights set on Yale.*

> *We divided our time between going for long walks, lingering over dinner in local restaurants, playing poker till all the hours, then going for more long walks to clear our heads . . .*

. . . or in this marvellous extract from Stefan Zweig's novella *Confusion:*

> *I have always had a horror of adultery, but not for any self-righteous moral reasons, not out of prudery and convention, not so much because taking possession of a strange body is theft committed in the dark, but because almost every woman will give away her husband's most intimate secrets at such moments.*

Consider also this sentence from Jamie Manners' book *The Seven Noses of Soho*:

Each side displays a carved coat of arms within a ziggurat gable, the door has a Gothic arch, and tiny octagonal railings crown the roof.

That comma after *arch* stops anyone from reading *a Gothic arch and tiny octagonal railings* in one breath and thinking, even for a moment, that the octagonal railings belong to the door. If the comma wasn't there, the reader might have to read the sentence twice to get the sense – and that's always faintly annoying.

The curators of an art exhibition I visited caused me just that low level of annoyance with a caption on the subject of a painting of a hunt: from 1660, hunting, they said, was . . .

. . . no longer the sole preserve of the aristocracy and wealthy burghers could also take part in it.

The fact that the line break fell where it did added to the confusion, but a comma after *aristocracy* or a semicolon (see page 85) instead of the *and* would have stopped me thinking that hunting was *no longer the sole preserve of the aristocracy and wealthy*.

And the lack of a comma makes this sentence, from a local newspaper, frankly ambiguous:

London has many options available to help budding cyclists get in the saddle, including quiet routes away from traffic and the Santander Cycle Hire scheme.

Does this mean that the Santander scheme is one of the options to help budding cyclists get in the saddle, or that there are quiet routes away from the scheme? Logic tells me the former (it helps that I know what the Santander scheme is); if I read it pedantically, with no knowledge of the context, I can't be sure. If I'm right, a comma after *traffic* would have made that clear, as would adjusting the word order. In other words, either

including quiet routes away from traffic, and the Santander Cycle Hire scheme

or

including the Santander Cycle Hire scheme and quiet routes away from traffic.

Similarly, a newspaper interview with the actor Jonny Lee Miller reported that he and Angelina Jolie had *wed a month after* Trainspotting *came out in a small ceremony.* My guess is that it was the wedding rather than the launch of *Trainspotting* that involved a small ceremony; again, commas or a change of word order would have removed the doubt:

. . . wed, a month after Trainspotting *came out, in a small ceremony*

. . . wed in a small ceremony a month after Trainspotting *came out.*

Apposition

Whether we know it or not, we're introduced to nouns in apposition at an early age. In my case it was thanks to Bill and Ben the Flowerpot Men; other generations might have known Champion the Wonder Horse, Noggin the Nog, Thomas the Tank Engine or Bob the Builder.

What it means is that a phrase or clause ('the flowerpot men', 'the wonder horse' and so on) expands on the meaning of the noun, answering questions such as 'Who are Bill and Ben?' or 'Which Noggin are you talking about?'

None of these examples requires punctuation, but they might do if you put them into a longer sentence:

> Bill and Ben, the flowerpot men, lived at the bottom of the garden.

> Champion, the wonder horse, was ridden by the singing cowboy Gene Autry.

What the commas indicate – and note that there are two of them – is that you are bracketing off the information from the rest of the sentence. You could, if you chose, have used parentheses or dashes instead:

> Bill and Ben (the flowerpot men) lived at the bottom of the garden.

> Champion – the wonder horse – was ridden by the singing cowboy Gene Autry.

If the expression came at the end of a sentence, you'd need only one comma:

Little Weed was the friend of Bill and Ben, the flowerpot men.

The same would be true at the end of a clause followed by a colon or semicolon:

Little Weed was the friend of Bill and Ben, the flowerpot men; they spent a lot of time together at the bottom of the garden.

Gene Autry rode Champion, the wonder horse; the two appeared together over 150 times.

But anywhere else, the commas, like dashes and parentheses, come in pairs. This can be important with what are called *non-restrictive* or *non-defining* clauses.

Little women

There's a subtle difference between *my daughter Jo* and *my daughter, Jo.* Consider:

My daughter, Jo, wanted to be a novelist.

The commas put the name into apposition – what you are saying is *my daughter, whose name is Jo and who is the only daughter I have.* Omit the commas and you have something different: *My daughter Jo wanted to be a novelist* could be followed by *while Meg thought she would like to teach.*

You could have any number of daughters; you haven't excluded that possibility.

Similarly:

My daughters, Jo and Beth, were great friends

tells us you have only two daughters. On the other hand:

My daughters Jo and Beth were great friends

doesn't exclude the possibility of others. You could add ... *but Meg kept herself to herself* or ... *but they didn't want to play with Amy.*

Note, though, that, as is very often the case, these commas come in pairs. *My daughter, Jo wanted to be a novelist* or *My daughters, Jo and Beth were great friends* would be wrong.

Restrictive and non-restrictive

It may seem perverse, but let's start by defining a *non-restrictive* or non-defining *clause*. It is one that gives extra, 'by the way' information. A *restrictive* or *defining clause* is essential to the sense, if not the grammar, of the sentence: without it, what you're saying will be incomplete or boring.

For example, in

The doctor who looked after me looked a bit like George Clooney

who looked after me is essential to the sentence: it's a defining clause. Without it, assuming no one has mentioned the doctor before, *the doctor looked a bit like George Clooney* leaves the reader wondering which doctor you are talking about. And perhaps worrying that you may be delirious.

On the other hand, in

The doctor, who looked a bit like George Clooney, looked after me

the fact that the doctor looked a bit like George Clooney is incidental to the sentence – the important thing is that he looked after you. So this is a *non-defining, non-restrictive* clause. It's almost as if it were in brackets: it needs to be 'cut off' from the rest of the sentence by a pair of commas.

In fact, if you omit these 'bracketing commas', you change the meaning: *The doctor who looked a bit like George Clooney looked after me* suggests that the doctor who looked like Jodie Whittaker was not assigned to your case.

If terms such as restrictive and non-restrictive feel a bit daunting, try remembering that a non-restrictive clause is 'by the way'. If it could easily be left out, you've added it for interest only, put commas round it.

When the subject of the restrictive or non-restrictive clause is a thing rather than a person, some people insist that the restrictive clause is introduced by *that* and the non-restrictive by *which*:

The dress that I longed to buy was red

The dress, which (by the way) *I longed to buy, was red*

Maybe, but this doesn't alter the fact that the non-restrictive clause needs commas.

To bracket or not to bracket

Here's an example – spotted in another art gallery – of a bracketing comma where it has no business to be:

> *The farm became a retreat for surrealist and avant-garde artists, most famously, Pablo Picasso.*

Remember that the point of bracketing commas is that you can lift out the bit they enclose and be left with something that makes sense. In this case, what remained would be:

> *The farm became a retreat for surrealist and avant-garde artists Pablo Picasso*

– which simply can't be right. What is required in the original sentence is a single comma after *artists*. This would divide the main clause (*The farm became a retreat for surrealist and avant-garde artists*) from the phrase *most famously Pablo Picasso*, four words that clearly go together and shouldn't have a comma breaking them up.

●

Other forms of parenthesis

To move away from commas for a moment, here's a 'by the way' section on … well, on other ways of saying 'by the way'.

When you put a pair of commas around a non-restrictive clause, you're creating what has been called a weak interruption. Sometimes, though, you'll want to make a stronger one, and for that you can introduce dashes or parentheses.

Most UK publishers and publications use what is called a *spaced en dash* – a line of the length just shown, with a space before and after it. American style tends to prefer the longer *em dash* — with or without spaces. (*Em* is an old printing measurement based on the amount of space taken up by a capital *M*, with an *en* being half an *em*.) So

Use whatever style you like – it doesn't matter

Use whatever style you like — it doesn't matter

Use whatever style you like—it doesn't matter

are all acceptable. A closed-up *en dash*-like this-isn't generally used because it looks too much like a hyphen.

If you're using dashes to isolate part of a sentence, there must be two of them:

All the colours of the rainbow – from red through to violet – were represented in her wardrobe.

My grandfather – always known as Pappy – was the dominant figure in my childhood.

If your 'interruption' comes at the end of the statement,

however, you need only one dash, because the full stop, semicolon, question mark or exclamation mark takes the place of the other:

Her wardrobe featured all the colours of the rainbow – from red through to violet.

The dominant figure in my childhood was my grandfather – always known as Pappy; at the age of eighty-eight he was as tall and handsome as ever.

We could go early – what do you think?

You can't do that – Mother would have a fit!

Parentheses make an even stronger interruption than dashes, and there must always be a pair of them, even at the end of a clause:

My grandfather (always known as Pappy) was the dominant figure in my childhood.

The dominant figure in my childhood was my grandfather (always known as Pappy); at the age of eighty-eight he was as tall and handsome as ever.

You can't use dashes or parentheses if your 'interruption' comes at the start of the sentence: *Always known as Pappy – my grandfather was the dominant figure in my childhood* and *(Always known as Pappy) my grandfather was the dominant figure in my childhood* are both wrong. For this sort of construction, you have to be content with a comma.

Dashes can be used to show that you are defining a term:

The use of chiaroscuro *– contrasting light and shadow – is a feature of Caravaggio's work.*

Each article is preceded by an abstract – a short summary of its content – which can be read without payment of a fee.

Stollen – a German fruit bread traditionally eaten at Christmas – was on offer on every market stall.

Parentheses would also be acceptable in those examples, and are the conventional way of isolating extra information or explanation, such as the dates of a historical event or a person's life or reign, the full version of an abbreviation or a translation of a foreign or technical term:

The American Civil War (1861–5)

Mahatma Gandhi (1869–1948)

The ANC (African National Congress)

Caveat emptor ('let the buyer beware')

The sleepwalking scene (Act V, scene i)

You could use dashes for the last three examples, but they would look odd in the first two, where you already have a dash linking the dates. Remember that the point of punctuation is to make something easier to read: you don't want to confuse your readers by putting in too many dashes – or too many brackets, come to that. If you have a complicated sentence that might require two lots of brackets, see if you can substitute dashes for one of them:

> *Edward VII – Queen Victoria's eldest son (reigned 1901–10) – was almost sixty when he came to the throne.*

Sometimes what you want to put in brackets is a whole sentence, in which case you have a choice of ways to punctuate it:

> *Steinbeck was never part of the literary establishment (they disapproved of his interest in poor immigrants).*
>
> *Steinbeck was never part of the literary establishment. (They disapproved of his interest in poor immigrants.)*

You may feel that there is a subtle difference between the two and you can choose the one that appeals to you more. Personally, I think that the first version flows more smoothly, but that doesn't mean that the second is 'wrong'. From the point of view of the punctuation, though, there are rules. If you choose the first option, you have only a partial sentence within the brackets, so it begins with a lower-case letter and the full stop goes *outside*. With the second option, there is a complete sentence, beginning with a capital and ending with a full stop, *inside* the brackets.

●

Square brackets

Square brackets – […] – are different from ordinary brackets or parentheses – (…) – in that they indicate that you, the author, are making an addition or an observation, usually to something that you are quoting. Say, for example, you were writing about John F. Kennedy and wanted to quote this sentence from the biography of the late President by Robert Dallek:

> *Although he conveyed a certain coolness or self-control, his radiant smile and genuine openness made him immediately likable.*

It is clear from Dallek's context that *he* means the President. But it might not be obvious from yours. So you might choose to write either

> *Although [Kennedy] conveyed a certain coolness or self-control, his radiant smile and genuine openness made him immediately likable*

or

> *Although he [Kennedy] conveyed a certain coolness or self-control, his radiant smile and genuine openness made him immediately likable.*

The first shows that you are replacing the original author's word(s) with one of your own; the second shows that you have kept Dallek's words but feel they need explanation.

Similarly, the words you are quoting may contain a term that might not be familiar to all your readers. Use square brackets for your explanation:

> *Dante's* Divine Comedy *is the oldest surviving example of* terza rima [a rhyming scheme that follows the pattern *aba bcb cdc* and so on].

Put square brackets around the word *sic* (Latin for 'thus') to indicate that you are quoting a mistake, but that the mistake was in the original and is not of your making; or that you are questioning an opinion expressed by the writer you are quoting:

> *Popeye and his wife Olive Oil* [sic].
>
> *Mark Twain wrote to his publisher, 'January and November* [sic] *didn't pan out as well as December.'*
>
> *The firm's loss for the year was given as £20,000* [sic].

In these examples the [*sic*] indicates that you know the character's surname is spelled *Oyl*; that this is indeed what Twain wrote, although it looks as if he might have meant *January and February*; and that the loss was more like £200,000, but that the report being quoted is misleading.

You wouldn't use parentheses in any of these contexts.

Co-ordination

Reverting to commas, use them to separate co-ordinate adjectives preceding a noun. Co-ordinate adjectives are those that describe a noun in the same way and are of equal importance:

a long, boring, bad-tempered board meeting

To assess whether or not adjectives are co-ordinate and therefore need commas, try:

- removing one or more of them

- replacing the comma with *and*

- reversing the order.

If you are left with something that makes sense, you have co-ordinate adjectives (though see the box opposite for more about the order of adjectives).

a long, boring, board meeting

a long and boring and bad-tempered board meeting

a long, bad-tempered, boring board meeting

All fine – keep the commas.

But how about *She wore a long red woollen coat and shabby leather boots?*

A red, woollen, long coat and leather shabby boots

is all wrong; *a long and red and woollen coat* is weird too. So these are what are called *cumulative adjectives* – they build on each other, producing a cumulative effect, and don't need commas.

If you are using commas in a list of adjectives, don't put one after the last, immediately before the noun: *a long, boring, bad-tempered, board meeting* and *a long, red, woollen, coat* are wrong.

The order of adjectives

As a general rule, a string of adjectives should go in this order:

- quantity or number
- quality or opinion
- size
- age
- shape
- colour
- nationality
- material

I have no recollection of learning this, although it is a formula taught to students of English as a second language. Perhaps it comes naturally to native speakers. We (apparently instinctively) write, for example,

Four beautiful little octagonal plates rather than *four octagonal beautiful little plates*

Lots of delicious Indian food rather than *Indian delicious lots of food*

A hideous old brown leather jacket rather than *an old leather hideous brown jacket*

If you want to use two adjectives from the same category, put *and* between them:

A hideous old brown and yellow (or brown-and-yellow) *leather jacket.*

If there are three, put a comma after the first one and *and* between the second and third:

A hideous old brown, yellow and orange leather jacket.

More than this and you may feel that you are providing too much information: just how much more hideous can this jacket get?

Some comma nitpicks and nuances

You might not have thought you could get excited by commas. But look at this sentence, from a short story called 'Ghosts' by Chimamanda Ngozi Adichie. The narrator, a retired university lecturer, is reminiscing about a former colleague:

It was he who, when the new vice chancellor, a Nigerian man raised in England, announced that all lecturers must

*wear ties to class, had defiantly continued to wear his brightly
coloured tunics.*

It's quite a complicated sentence, but if you read it aloud, pausing briefly at each comma, it falls beautifully into place. The main statement is *It was he who had defiantly continued to wear his brightly coloured tunics.* The commas after *who* and *class* show that everything between them is to be treated as a parenthesis. But the commas after *chancellor* and *England* create a parenthesis within that parenthesis, separating the 'by the way' description of the new vice chancellor – *a Nigerian man raised in England* – from the more important statement that he announced that all lecturers must wear ties to class. You could substitute dashes for this second pair of commas:

*It was he who, when the new vice chancellor – a Nigerian
man raised in England – announced that all lecturers must
wear ties to class, had defiantly continued to wear his
brightly coloured tunics.*

But Adichie is very sparing in her use of dashes. She's preferred to stick to commas, and to position them meticulously.

Another example, this time from Ian Rankin's novel *Hide and Seek*:

*The psychologist, Dr Poole, who wasn't really a psychologist,
but rather, he had explained, a lecturer in psychology, quite a*

different thing, studied the photographs carefully.

If you read this aloud, giving the same weight of pause to each comma, it sounds rather breathless. You might have preferred:

*The psychologist, Dr Poole – who wasn't really a
psychologist, but rather, he had explained, a lecturer
in psychology, quite a different thing – studied the
photographs carefully.*

Or:

*The psychologist, Dr Poole, who wasn't really a
psychologist, but rather – he had explained – a lecturer
in psychology, quite a different thing, studied the
photographs carefully.*

Or even:

*The psychologist, Dr Poole – who wasn't really a
psychologist, but rather, he had explained, a lecturer
in psychology (quite a different thing) – studied the
photographs carefully.*

The dashes and parentheses demand longer pauses than the commas, but presumably that isn't what the author wanted. Somehow, the breathlessness of the sentence helps to convey the pomposity with which Dr Poole has explained his credentials.

Those were the nuances; now for the nitpicks. An obituary of the actor Gene Wilder reported that *his favorite*

[sic] *comedians, Bill Murray, Dan Aykroyd and John Belushi all appeared in a* Saturday Night Live *skit*. Interpret this strictly according to the punctuation and you will see a list with four entries in it:

- his favourite comedians
- Bill Murray
- Dan Aykroyd
- John Belushi

In other words, Murray, Aykroyd and Belushi do not feature among his favourite comedians. This is clearly not what was intended. It should have read:

> *His favorite comedians, Bill Murray, Dan Aykroyd and John Belushi, all appeared . . .*

… with the commas after *comedians* and *Belushi* forming the parenthesis. Or, for the absolute avoidance of ambiguity and of a glut of commas:

> *His favorite comedians – Bill Murray, Dan Aykroyd and John Belushi – all appeared . . .*

An advertisement for masaltos.com, offering 'elevator shoes for men', boasted:

*Thanks to these Italian shoes, men can discreetly add up
to 7 cm, or 2.75 inches to their height.*

OK, they can add 2.75 inches to their height, but what are
they adding the 7 cm to? I think we should perhaps not
be told. A comma after inches would have left no room
for innuendo, but would have shown that 2.75 inches was
merely another way of expressing 7 cm and that the shoes
could add either measurement to your height. In fact, the *or*
is the real culprit here: *7 cm (2.75 inches)* or *7 cm/2.75 inches*
would have shown more clearly that the two measurements
were interchangeable.

And, to raise the tone slightly, an article about a painting
by Frederic Leighton said:

*In 1915 [Vernon Watney] wrote to Charles Bell, the keeper
of the Ashmolean Museum offering* Flaming June *on loan.*

A comma after *Museum* would have told us – accurately
– that Bell was the keeper of the Ashmolean and that
Watney, who owned the painting, was offering it to him. Its
absence means that we read *the keeper of the Ashmolean
Museum offering* Flaming June *on loan* in one breath and
can be forgiven for thinking that Bell was offering to lend
the painting to some unspecified beneficiary.

And finally, just give me a moment . . .

You could (at a pinch) summarize the comma's function as telling the reader where to pause for breath. Or perhaps simply *allowing* the reader to pause for breath. Read this sentence, from a wonderful book called *Bookshops* by the Spanish academic Jorge Carrión. In the previous paragraph he has listed a number of bookshops, so *the first* refers to one of them:

> The history of the first goes back to the middle of the nineteenth century at the height of the Gold Rush when in 1853 the Swabian traveller Anton Roman started selling books and musical instruments to miners in Shasta City at the Shasta Book Store opposite the El Dorado Hotel.

There's nothing you could pinpoint as being wrong, but it's five lines without a breather. I can't help feeling that the addition of three commas would have made the reader's life easier:

> The history of the first goes back to the middle of the nineteenth century, at the height of the Gold Rush, when in 1853 the Swabian traveller Anton Roman started selling books and musical instruments to miners in Shasta City, at the Shasta Book Store opposite the El Dorado Hotel.

Professor Carrión likes complex sentences, and that is his privilege. But here is one – only slightly shorter and taken from the same paragraph – where he has given the reader every possible assistance:

> *However, on my first visit to San Francisco, I went on a devout pilgrimage to City Lights because I still believed in my invisible passport; when I returned ten years later and they took me to Clement Street, I felt I was gaining something I would never lose.*

It includes a pair of bracketing commas indicating an 'aside'; a semicolon showing the ending of something that could have been a sentence, but isn't the end of the thought; and a comma separating an introductory clause from a main clause. It all just helps.

~

4

Things That Clarify: III

Hyphen (-): *the punctuation mark used to separate the parts of some compound words and to link the words of a phrase. It may indicate that two or more words have been made into one, either permanently (as in* deaf-mute *or* home-made*) or temporarily, particularly when a phrase is to be used attributively, as a description of another noun (as in* sought-after location *or* user-friendly software*).*

The hyphen, that mini-dash, shorter even than an en (see page 48), that appears in compound words, is often overlooked, often poo-pooed, but it punches above its weight when it comes to making meaning clear. That said, it's extraordinarily difficult to be categorical about when to use a hyphen to create a compound word, when to write a single word or when to use two or more. Extraordinarily difficult because:

- there is often little logic to it, although those who work with words may say they have a 'feel' for the rights and wrongs of individual cases; and
- not even the experts agree.

Take, for example, the many compounds – nouns, adjectives and verbs – beginning with 'house'. My *Collins English Dictionary* gives *housebound* ('unable to leave one's house because of illness, injury, etc.'), *household* ('the people living together in one house collectively'), *houseleek* ('a plant of the genus *Sempervivum*'), *housekeeper*, *housemaster* and even *househusband* as single words, but the birds *house martin* and *house sparrow*, together with *house lights* ('the lights in the auditorium of a theatre, cinema, etc.') and *house plant* as two. It is sparing with its hyphens: *house-broken, house-proud, house-train* and *house-warming* are the only common expressions to which it allocates one.

Looking at this list, you may say that the tendency is for nouns to be one word, verbs and adjectives to be hyphenated, but what is the rationale behind hyphenating *house-proud* but not *housebound*?

It gets worse. The *Oxford English Reference Dictionary* (OERD) hyphenates *house-martin*, but writes *house sparrow* as two words; Chambers has both as two words; it also gives *house leek*, but – in common with the OERD – *house-husband*. And these examples are taken from just a column or two of dictionaries that run to well over a thousand pages. Flip through those same tomes and you'll find differences of opinion over terms as diverse as *half term*, *roller coaster* and *antifreeze*.

So what can we learn from this? Well, *house-husband* (however you choose to write it) raises a relevant point. People of my generation may remember it being used rather disparagingly of John Lennon in his New York/Yoko Ono years, when he seemed to have given up song-writing. (Or should that be songwriting? Again, my sources differ.) At the time – the late 1970s – the idea of a man staying at home to look after the kids and deal with the domestic stuff was something of a novelty, so we might imagine that *house-husband* was coined specifically to describe the way the former Beatle was living.

Not so. The OED online gives a citation from 1858:

A crowd of house-husbands—if the term be admissible in default of house-wives—sauntering along among the crockery-stalls in search of pots and pans.

This is taken from a novel set in Ancient Greece and written by an English politician called Edward Aldam Leatham. By hyphenating *house-husbands*, the author is drawing attention to the fact that it is a combination of two separate words, not an established term. Indeed, the context and the fact that there is no earlier record of it make it likely that he made it up for the occasion – what is sometimes called a *nonce word*, suitable for the present moment but not intended to be used again. It's worth noting that he hyphenates *house-wives*, too, although *housewife* (as one word) had already been around for 600 years. What does this tell us? That Mr Leatham had a particular affection for hyphens? (The appearance of one in *crockery-stalls*, where it doesn't feel entirely necessary, lends weight to this theory.) Or that, having hyphenated his new coinage, he felt obliged, for the sake of consistency, to hyphenate its more familiar counterpart? Either or both could be true.

The Victorians certainly liked hyphens. Jane Austen's nephew Edward Austen Leigh, composing a biography of his aunt not long after Edward Leatham was writing about Ancient Greece, had occasion to mention the joys of spring in the country, including early primroses, anemones and *the first bird's-nest*. That hyphen makes it absolutely clear that he means the first nest (of the season) belonging to a bird, rather than a nest belonging to the first bird. A bit over-precise, you might think, but he was an elderly clergyman and over-precision was probably his stock-in-trade. He also hyphenates *bed-room* (not to mention *ball-room*, *dining-room* and *sitting-room*), though his aunt had written *bedroom* in both *Sense and Sensibility* and *Northanger Abbey* some half-century earlier. Let's write Mr Austen Leigh off as a bit of a pedant and go back to house-husbands.

Whether or not Edward Leatham coined the term, other

people picked it up and used it. When this happens, new coinages evolve into familiar, established expressions – so much so that their origins may be forgotten and the need for a hyphen may disappear. The OED online hyphenates *song-bird*, as do all six of its citations, dating from 1774 to 1896; all my more recent dictionaries give it as one word, with no suggestion that it has ever been otherwise. Early uses of *off beat* – referring to a beat of music that is usually unstressed, but that may be stressed in some jazz and rock styles – are inconsistent: one word, two words, a hyphenated word all seem to have been acceptable. But when we come to the non-musical meaning of *eccentric* or *unconventional*, the musical origins are forgotten and the single word *offbeat* is near universal.

There are many, many more examples, from all walks of life. The most obvious modern one is *email* – now so much a part of our daily lives that we barely recall that the *e* is an abbreviation of *electronic* and until quite recently we were writing *'e-mail'* or even *'e'-mail*. Those inverted commas are an additional indication of an unfamiliar term, distancing the writer from what he has written. It's almost as if he wanted to say *the so-called e-mail* but decided that was a bit disparaging (see page 146, Distance Quotes, for more about this).

Now you see them . . .

P. G. Wodehouse was another author who liked hyphens. Writing about tennis in the 1930s he hyphenates both *back-*

hand and *tennis-court*, which nowadays would generally be written as one word and two respectively. But then he also hyphenates *right-angle*, *top-hat*, *ham-sandwich* and *beef-steak* (though not all in the essay about tennis – the beef-steak occurs in a discussion of what he would feed his kestrel if he happened to own one).

More recently, I noticed – in a novel by a Scottish author first published in 1987 – hyphens in *bus-fare*, *wall-space*, *picture-book*, *field-day*, *toffee-apple*, *fairy-tale*. All of these, to my eye, looked a little odd.

Thinking that the Scots may have their own rules about this, as about many other things, I looked them up in Chambers, historically a Scottish-based dictionary. The only one it hyphenates is *picture-book*; the others are given as two words, except *bus fare*, which doesn't appear at all (although both *bus lane* and *bus pass* appear as two words). The only conclusion I can draw is that that particular author, too, has a (slightly old-fashioned) taste for hyphens.

I say old-fashioned because hyphens are being used less and less: I don't think many of us would bat an eyelid to see *picturebook* or *fairytale* written as one word, although as I type this, Word has put a red squiggle under both.

Even odder, I felt, was something I spotted in a novel published in 1996 and not written by a Scot: a hyphen in *we'd better get a move-on*. He's taken an idiomatic verbal phrase – *to get a move on*, of course, means to hurry – and turned part of it into a noun, as if a *move-on* were something you could *get*, like a grip on the situation or a skinny cappuccino.

All of this shows, unhelpfully, that there is a lot of idiosyncrasy and a certain amount of fashion about the use of hyphens. In the absence of hard and fast rules, therefore, we have to rely on the following general principles:

- use hyphens as little as possible, but
- always use them if the alternative is ambiguous, and
- if a compound word when run together without a hyphen looks odd, is hard to decipher or hard to pronounce, put the hyphen back in.

That isn't what I meant

Putting two words together (with or without a hyphen) can subtly change their meaning. *A half term*, to revert to an example mentioned earlier, is, on the face of it, 50 per cent of a term. But *half-term* or *halfterm* has come to mean the brief holiday that occurs halfway through a term. Similarly, the novelist Peter May, writing about a rural community in the Outer Hebrides, describes *whitehouses* and *blackhouses*: the former 'built in the twenties of stone and lime'; the latter having 'dry-stone walls with thatched roofs'. There's no doubt that the whitehouses were white and the blackhouses black, but in both cases running the two words together adds a meaning that is concerned with more than colour. The difference is even more marked when it comes to a *greenhouse*, which is usually made of clear glass – green only if you let it go mouldy – and was originally called green because it was used to grow greenery.

Come to think of it, *dry-stone walls* are different from *dry stone walls*: the former are of a particular type built without mortar; the latter may or may not have mortar but haven't been rained on lately.

●

If you won't cooperate

Modern dictionaries routinely spell *cooperate* thus, but to my mind it's an occasion when we should hold out for the hyphen. There isn't a word 'coop-erate', suggesting something that a cooper or barrel-maker might do, but at first glance it's easy to assume that that is how *cooperate* should be pronounced. *Co-operate* makes it clear that the idea is to *operate* together (assuming we know that the *co-* indicates togetherness). Certainly if you abbreviate the word to give the name of a grocery chain or other co-operative enterprise, it's worth ensuring that readers don't imagine the *Coop* is somewhere you keep the hens.

Similar arguments apply to *co-opt* and *co-ordinate*, although with other repeated vowels, such as *pre-eminent* or *semi-independent*, the consensus seems to be in favour of maintaining the hyphen.

There are other words with other prefixes where the hyphen avoids ambiguity:

- *Predate* is the verb associated with predation or

preying on something; to *pre-date* is to come before.

- *Recreation* is a leisure activity; *re-creation*, should you be a god having second thoughts, is creating again. To *recount* is to tell a tale; *re-counting* is what you do after a close election. To *recover* something is to get it back; to *re-cover* is to put a new cover on a book or an armchair.

Remember, we're talking about the written word here. You aren't going to be there to explain to your readers what you mean and they won't have intonation or difference in stress to help them out. Do them a favour. Write clearly.

Something that actually is a rule

Use a hyphen, say the textbooks, if the root word starts with a capital and you are attaching a prefix to it: *anti-American*, *pre-Columbian*, *pan-European*, *post-Marxist*.

If you're attaching prefixes such as these to an adjective that doesn't have a capital, the resulting compound adjective needs either to be hyphenated or to be written as a single word. In other words:

pre-lunch drinks could be *prelunch*, but they mustn't be *pre lunch*.

post-war Vietnam could be *postwar*, but not *post war* (which could suggest a war about the mail, or about something to do with fences).

non-toxic chemicals could be *nontoxic* but not *non toxic*.

anti-war demonstrators could be *antiwar*, but not *anti war*.

I prefer hyphens in all these examples, but they are often omitted in today's hyphen-averse world.

Compound adjectives

With compound nouns, you can argue that it doesn't matter much: the meaning is clear and that's what counts. This can sometimes be the case with compound adjectives, too.

Sometimes. Not always.

If you're writing about *a light blue car*, for example, you're much more likely to be describing its colour (*a light-blue car*) than assessing its weight (*a light, blue car*). But what about an item of clothing? *A light blue jacket* could be made of some flimsy material, in any tint from baby blue to navy (*a light, blue jacket*); *a light-blue jacket* is definitely of a delicate hue, but gives no clue as to the fabric.

Similarly, *a shocking pink dress* could be a subtle shade but very low cut. *A shocking-pink dress* is eye-catching because of its colour, not because of the amount of bosom it displays.

I also read about somebody working on a building site wearing *a hard steel front boot*. It tempts the reader to speculate as to the texture and material of his back boot. What was meant was *a hard, steel-front boot*.

The great food writer Elizabeth David once referred to *the rich wine dark sauce* of an octopus stew, which at first glance is (no pun intended) a mouthful. The recipe certainly contains red wine, so has she missed out an *and*? Should it be *the rich wine and (the) dark sauce*? Or has she got the words in the wrong order and meant the *rich, dark, wine sauce*? No. A simple hyphen, and perhaps a comma, too, would have turned this unambiguously into the *rich, wine-dark sauce* – a sauce that was rich in flavour and dark in colour thanks to the wine.

If you choose to do without hyphens, your readers may not be sure whether *thirteen year old girls* are teenagers or babies, and whether *hang glider pilots in training* is a warning to avoid low-flying craft, an exclamation of impatience or an instruction to execute any pilot who hasn't passed the exams yet. And they may wonder if a *high spirited adventure* requires the use of a tightrope and/or recreational drugs.

Just after I finished writing this, an unsolicited advertisement popped up on my email page. It read, in its entirety and allocating a single word to each line:

Stress
Free
Official
Parking

Was it offering me official parking that would cause me no stress, or instructing me to emphasize (to some unspecified third party) that there was official parking that didn't have to be paid for?

And what about *cross functional professionals,* spotted by a friend who works in the dark recesses of further education? A hyphen in *cross-functional* would have indicated that the professionals worked as, perhaps, both teachers and administrators; the lack of it suggests that they can do their jobs but are grumpy about it.

●

Another rule about hyphens

Compound adjectives beginning with *well* should be hyphenated if they precede the noun: *a well-groomed horse, a well-mannered child, a well-preserved monument*. But in similar constructions it's wrong to put a hyphen after an adverb ending in *-ly*: *a happily married couple, a hotly contested race, a newly minted coin, a thinly veiled excuse*. There's no way these expressions can be ambiguous, so a hyphen would serve no purpose. Leave it out.

Also leave the hyphen out of constructions such as *the horse was well groomed, the child was well mannered* and so on.

A hyphenation convention

Two-word numbers from *twenty-one* to *ninety-nine* are hyphenated, either on their own or as part of larger numbers:

Forty-one, forty-three and forty-seven are all prime numbers.

Thirty-six, forty-nine and sixty-four are perfect squares.

One hundred and forty-four is also a square; three hundred and forty-three is a cube.

Don't add extra hyphens unless you are forming a compound adjective in constructions such as *a hundred-and-forty-four-year sentence.*

Hanging hyphens

While a hyphen is usually used to connect two words, you sometimes see one left hanging in a phrase where two compound adjectives are involved.

Eh?

Sorry. Here's an example.

If you were writing an article about healthy eating, you might well refer to *vitamin-rich foods*. Or, indeed, *mineral-rich foods*. Foods that are rich in those desirable commodities. But you might find it more convenient to put them in the same phrase and call them *vitamin- and mineral-rich foods*. That loose hyphen after *vitamin* indicates that *rich* belongs to it, too.

Similarly, a gardener might refer to *early- and late-flowering clematis*; an economist to *low- and middle-income sectors of society*; a school prospectus to *11- to 16-year-olds*; a baker to *chocolate- and orange-flavoured muffins* (in the last example, a second hyphen would change the meaning – *chocolate-and-orange-flavoured muffins* would be one style of muffin containing both flavours; the hanging hyphen shows you've gone to the trouble of baking two batches and keeping the flavours separate).

Less common, but equally valid, is a hanging hyphen at the start of a word: *Rhesus-positive and -negative blood* refers to two different types of blood, one containing the Rhesus factor, the other lacking it. You might argue that leaving out that second hyphen would confuse no one, there being no such thing as negative blood, but purists would maintain it was correct.

A note on scientific terms

I find it interesting that hyphens seem to disappear more quickly from any remotely scientific or technical terms. *Healthcare*, *backup*, *timelapse*, *audiovisual* are all words for which you could make a case for hyphenation, but they are all frequently seen (rightly or wrongly) as one word. I even recently saw *postneonatal*, which might arguably contain two hyphens, but is widely used – on the internet at least – as a single word, to describe an infant between the ages of one and twelve months, so *post* (after) the *neonatal* (newborn) stage.

I have no explanation for this. My best guesses are that writers of technical texts assume that their readers will understand what they are talking about; or that scientists are too busy splitting the atom (or whatever it is that scientists do these days) to bother about mere punctuation . . .

Still think none of this matters much? Well, I recently read a reference to the hyphenless *light sabre duel* between Luke Skywalker and Darth Vader. It's a while since I saw *The Empire Strikes Back*, but I seem to remember that that duel was pretty heavy. And the cookery book *Leon Fast & Free* by Jane Baxter and John Vincent – aimed at those who want to avoid sugar, gluten, dairy products and the like – has the subtitle *Free-from recipes for people who really like food*. Try leaving the hyphen out of that.

~

5

Things That Make You Look Good

Semicolon

Semicolon (;): *the punctuation mark used to indicate a pause that is midway between a comma and a full stop.*

One of the first 'set books' I ever studied at school was *Great Expectations*. In only the third paragraph, at the bottom of the first page, was this extraordinary sentence:

At such a time I found out for certain that this bleak place overgrown with nettles was the churchyard; and that Philip Pirrip, late of this parish, and also Georgiana wife of the above, were dead and buried; and that Alexander,

Bartholomew, Abraham, Tobias, and Roger, infant children of the aforesaid, were also dead and buried; and that the dark flat wilderness beyond the churchyard, intersected with dikes and mounds and gates, with scattered cattle feeding on it, was the marshes; and that the low leaden line beyond was the river; and that the distant savage lair from which the wind was rushing was the sea; and that the small bundle of shivers growing afraid of it all and beginning to cry, was Pip.

I don't suppose for a minute that I experienced a punctuational epiphany on reading this. I must have been about thirteen; I expect I turned the page and got on with the story. It was only in later life that I went back to it and thought, 'Wow.' A hundred and twenty-four words in a single sentence: an otherwise unswallowable mouthful made digestible by six semicolons.

The point of a semicolon is to indicate a break that is more substantial than a comma but doesn't justify a full stop. Dickens could have divided that paragraph into seven shortish sentences (or two or three medium-sized ones), but he'd have lost the continuity, the cumulative effect, the feeling that this is all one connected thought flowing through a small boy's mind. In fact, the sentence is a sort of list, with each semicolon separating one of the things that Pip found out for certain.

Isn't this all a bit subtle?

Well yes, but once you get into it, it can be quite fun. Here's a statement that could be punctuated in a number of ways and shows the delicate distinctions between them:

You couldn't tell me anything: I was fifteen and I was sure I knew it all.

You couldn't tell me anything – I was fifteen and I was sure I knew it all.

You couldn't tell me anything. I was fifteen and I was sure I knew it all.

You couldn't tell me anything; I was fifteen and I was sure I knew it all.

None of these is incorrect.

The colon (as we shall see a bit later) has an 'explanatory' function: the *reason* you couldn't tell me anything is that I was fifteen and sure I knew it all.

The dash serves the same purpose – it's just a bit less formal.

The full stop creates two sentences, which you may feel produces a slightly staccato effect. But, hey. Your role model may be Ernest Hemingway. Staccato may be what you want.

The semicolon divides the two clauses, but the separation isn't as definite as if you'd used a full stop. What the semicolon *doesn't* do is express the sense of 'because' – it gives you two separate statements of fact, without suggesting that one is the result of the other. It's a tiny distinction, but that's where the questions of style and taste come in.

Travelling by train recently I noticed on the electronic display:

Please stand clear of the doors, this train is ready to leave.

It seemed to me that that was almost the only incorrect way the sentence could have been punctuated:

Please stand clear of the doors: this train is ready to leave

Please stand clear of the doors – this train is ready to leave

Please stand clear of the doors. This train is ready to leave

Please stand clear of the doors; this train is ready to leave

would all have been acceptable, with the same subtle differences as in my *you couldn't tell me anything* example. Or they could have added a short conjunction, to give

Please stand clear of the doors, as this train is ready to leave.

I'd have been happy with that.

You may think this sort of pedantry is wasted on train announcements and you may be right. But the train company had already cancelled the train I was supposed to be catching and made me late: I was in no mood to give them the benefit of the doubt. Plus I'm writing a book about punctuation and I get a bit obsessed.

But it can be useful too

Like commas (see page 38), semicolons can help us make sense of items in a list. A recent magazine article listed some of the works of psychoanalyst Adam Phillips:

> *Missing Out: In Praise of the Unlived Life, On Kissing, Tickling and Being Bored* and *Monogamy.*

That colon tells us that *In Praise of the Unlived Life* 'belongs' to *Missing Out* – it's a subtitle. The second *and* being in roman type when everything else is in italics indicates that it is not part of a title, so we can be confident that one of the works is called simply *Monogamy*. But what about the rest of it? Is *On Kissing, Tickling and Being Bored* one title, or is there a work called *On Kissing* and another called *Tickling and Being Bored*? Assessing the punctuation alone, there is no way of telling.

Further research revealed that *On Kissing, Tickling and Being Bored* is the title of a collection of essays (which I must order as soon as I have finished writing this). A couple of semicolons – *Missing Out: In Praise of the Unlived Life*; *On Kissing, Tickling and Being Bored*; and *Monogamy* – would have made the list unambiguous.

Here's an example of a semicolon being used in another such list: this is from J. G. Farrell's novel *Troubles*, in which the Majestic is a once-glamorous hotel that has burned down:

> *Here and there among the foundations one might still find evidence of the Majestic's former splendour: the great number of cast-iron bathtubs, for instance, which had tumbled from one blazing floor to another until they hit*

the earth; twisted bed-frames also, some of them not yet
altogether rusted away; and a simply prodigious number of
basins and lavatory bowls.

This is John Betjeman, writing about railway architecture:

There are bridges: the Britannia Bridge over the Menai Strait,
by Robert Stephenson and Francis Thompson (1845–50),
with its guardian lions and cyclopean piers and entrances;
Conway Bridge in the Gothic style by the same architects,
blending with the castle; Brunel's wonderful brick bridge over
the Thames at Maidenhead with its nearly flat arches.

Both masterly examples, like the one from *Great Expectations* at the start of this chapter, of how semicolons can make sense of what might otherwise be long, rambling sentences.

And finally, from Reginald Hill's *The Death of Dalziel*, an example I have included simply because I love the idea of a greedy man in a coma, fighting for his life, having a fantasy like this:

. . . on one table crowns of lamb, barons of beef, loins of
pork ridged with crackling, honey-glazed hams; on another
roasted geese, Christmas turkeys, duck with cherries, pheasant
adorned with their own feathers; on a third whole salmon,
pickled herring, mountain ranges of oysters and mussels.

Using a semicolon

As a general rule, a semicolon follows a clause with a subject and a finite verb, and if it does so it must also be followed by a clause with a subject and a finite verb. It could often be replaced by *and* or *but* (or, if you wanted to show off, *whereas*) without substantially changing the meaning. Here's an example from William Boyd's *Any Human Heart*, in which a character, having moved away from New York, is sorting out his affairs from a distance:

> *Letters were written to friends; Helma packed up his apartment under his instructions, sold his furniture, crated up his possessions and had them shipped to London.*

And here's the poet Simon Armitage in a northern English village with an unusual name:

> *Bellingham-pronounced-Bellinjam is still dozing: condensation clings to the two police cars parked outside the stone-built station; a faulty light in the cashpoint machine flickers on and off; two old-fashioned petrol pumps straight out of an episode of* Heartbeat *stand like saluting sentries in the forecourt of a local garage.*

Again, we're looking at passages that could have been broken up into shorter sentences, but that would have been more abrupt, less elegant, if they had been.

On the other hand, here's an author trying hard but getting it wrong:

Matthew and Luke are likely to be translating this Aramaic word, giving it different nuances; 'debts' in Matthew and 'failings' in Luke.

The problem here is that there is no verb after the semicolon. It should be a colon, indicating that a list (admittedly a short one) is to follow. There's more about colons and lists a little later (see page 90).

Alternatively, if the author had had a hankering after a semicolon, he could have written:

Matthew and Luke are likely to be translating this Aramaic word, giving it different nuances; it appears as 'debts' in Matthew and 'failings' in Luke.

The second part of the sentence is now a complete main clause, so the semicolon is okay.

I said a general rule . . .

An exception to this finite-verb-after-a-semicolon business comes if you are using sentence fragments. In other words, if there isn't a verb before the semicolon, there doesn't need to be one afterwards. Look at these examples:

To understand this, we need to go further back in time.

*Back before the French Revolution; before even the
English Civil War.*

*Because of its timing, the New Hampshire primary is
highly significant. More so than the earlier Iowa caucus;
perhaps even more so than the larger California primary.*

And one from *Lord of the Flies* by William Golding:

*Once more, from a distance, he heard Jack's whisper.
'Scared?'
Not scared so much as paralysed; hung up here immovable
on the top of a diminishing, moving mountain.*

The point is that what comes after the semicolon takes
the same form as what comes before. In the first example,
two phrases beginning *before*; in the second, two phrases
beginning *more so than*; in the third, two fragments
describing the position the character is in.

The accidental comma

A comma can be used to link two sentences if it is followed
by *and*, *but*, *or*, *while* or *yet*.

A semicolon comes before other linking words such
as *however*, *therefore*, *nevertheless*, *meanwhile* and
consequently.

The distinction is that, with the first group, what follows
the punctuation is not a stand-alone sentence; in the second
group, it is. Thus:

*My son is going to Japan for the summer, and I plan to
join him for a week or so.*

You may go if you want to, but I'm staying at home.

*You had better be home by eleven, or your father will be
furious.*

*Darts remains as popular as ever, while other traditional
pub games are dying out.*

*We promoted the event on social media, yet no one
seemed very interested.*

You could re-punctuate some of these examples by leaving
out the conjunction and replacing the comma with a
semicolon:

*My son is going to Japan for the summer; I plan to join
him for a week or so.*

You may go if you want to; I'm staying at home.

*Darts remains as popular as ever; other traditional pub
games are dying out.*

And in at least the first three examples you could argue for
leaving out the comma altogether. What you couldn't do
is make a direct substitution, replacing the comma with a
semicolon. All the following would be wrong:

*My son is going to Japan for the summer; and I plan to
join him for a week or so.*

You may go if you want to; but I'm staying at home.

You had better be home by eleven; or your father will be furious.

Darts remains as popular as ever; while other traditional pub games are dying out.

We promoted the event on social media; yet no one seemed very interested.

Let's return to that second group of connecting words, the ones that *can* follow a semicolon:

My son is going to Japan for the summer; however, I can't join him for more than a week or so.

She failed to get home by eleven; therefore, her father was furious.

You may go if you want to; nevertheless, I'm staying at home.

Darts remains as popular as ever; meanwhile, other traditional pub games are dying out.

We promoted the event on social media; consequently, we sold all the tickets in two hours.

Another way of explaining it is that you could replace those semicolons with a full stop and capital letter:

However, I can't join him for more than a week or so

Nevertheless, I'm staying at home

Meanwhile, other traditional pub games are dying out

Therefore, her father was furious

Consequently, we sold all the tickets in two hours

are all grammatically sound and they all make sense. So they can follow a semicolon.

●

So what is the difference between a colon and a semicolon?

Colon (:): *the punctuation mark usually preceding an explanation or an example of what has gone before; also preceding a list or an extended quotation.*

It's worth repeating, I think, that a semicolon, like a full stop, is merely a pause. It divides one statement from another. With a colon, you are introducing the concept of cause and effect: what follows the colon is an explanation or an example of what has gone before. There's also no need to worry about finite verbs and which conjunctions you can use.

Easier to give some examples, perhaps.

In his book *The Seven Noses of Soho*, Jamie Manners describes an old-style East End café as having walls that are *panelled with beautiful marquetry: rising suns around the counter and art-deco fan shapes elsewhere.* That colon precedes a short list (of the two styles of marquetry). It suggests, 'When I say there is beautiful marquetry, what I mean is …' If Jamie had had a fancy to use a semicolon he could have written *[the walls are] panelled with beautiful marquetry; rising suns surround the counter and there are art-deco fan shapes elsewhere*. The bit following the semicolon could stand as a sentence in its own right, but would be a bit abrupt; using a semicolon rather than a full stop maintains the link between the *existence* of the marquetry and the *description* of it.

Here's another:

> *Alison could see herself being drawn into the net: she didn't want to be friends with these people, but there seemed no way out.*

Her not wanting to be friends but seeing no way out is an *explanation* of how she was being drawn into the net.

At the beginning of 2017, comedian Katherine Ryan was one of those quoted in a newspaper feature predicting what comedy would be like in the coming year:

> *There will be two main genres of comedy in 2017: that which has a point of view and that which does not.*

The colon says, 'The two main genres to which I am referring are …', but it says it rather more succinctly.

A colon can also be used if you're writing in a slightly terse, clipped style, as in this example from a detective story in which one policeman is explaining the circumstances to another:

> *'The murdered man . . . bought Lexham Manor some years*
> *ago. Sort of show-place: oak panelling, and that kind of thing.*
> *Cost a packet: never could make out why he wanted it.'*

Or in this colloquialism:

> *Old Tommy Cooper joke: man walks into a pub with a lump*
> *of asphalt on his shoulder . . .*

Again, the piece after the colon explains what has gone before. You could have written *There's an old Tommy Cooper joke that begins . . .*, but in this context (and particularly if you remember Tommy Cooper and are imitating his style) that would be a bit verbose. (The punchline, by the way, is *He says to the barman, 'Give me a pint, and one for the road.'*)

Subtitles

Colons are a boon to the creators of newspaper headlines and of television subtitles. As I write this, today's *Times* offers me *Sett for life: how badger colonies will be protected along HS2 line* and *Age of the flexitarian: millions now only eat meat at weekends*, while the 'Home!' section of the magazine (and I'll gloss quickly over the utter meaninglessness of that exclamation mark) has an article on *The art of upsizing: more space to show off those Damien Hirst paintings and classic Eames chairs.*

$\longrightarrow$

The television listings over the last week have included:

Thailand: Earth's Tropical Paradise; *Robson Crusoe: A Surprising Adventure*; *Britain's Ancient Capital: Secrets of Orkney*; *Walesa: Man of Hope* and *Martin Clunes: Islands of Australia*. I was slightly baffled by that last one because, so far as I am aware, Martin Clunes is not the name of an island of Australia. Perhaps the programme-makers rejected the idea of *Martin Clunes's Islands of Australia* because they were worried about where the apostrophe should go and how many s's they would need.

To sum up: (but not ;)

Two final examples of colon vs semicolon, both from travel pieces by the journalist Brian Jackman. First, when the building of a barrage across a river caused the fields to flood and ruined crops:

> *Farmers blamed the barrage; the water authorities blamed the weather.*

You could replace the punctuation with *but* or *whereas*, and there is no suggestion of cause and effect – the water authorities didn't blame the weather *because* the farmers blamed the barrage. So it's a semicolon.

Second, glancing skyward to see a bird of prey:

> *It was a goshawk: a powerful, barrel-chested hunter revered by falconers.*

The first part has a verb, the second part does not, so no semicolon. Also, the second part is an explanation of the first, hence the colon.

~

6

Things That Show Emotion

You may not think the punctuation can convey feelings, but, if so, I can assure you that you are missing out on a treat. None of the examples in this chapter really change meaning, but they certainly change tone.

Exclamation marks

Exclamation mark (!): *the punctuation mark used after exclamations and vehement commands, or for various other purposes such as drawing attention to an obvious mistake.*

The American writer F. Scott Fitzgerald is alleged to have deplored the use of exclamation marks, likening them to laughing at your own jokes. I wouldn't ban them quite so wholeheartedly, but then I have been known to laugh at my own jokes, so perhaps I am not the best arbiter. What I would say is that in any remotely formal writing – basically anything more formal than an SMS or WhatsApp communication – they should be used sparingly. Using an exclamation mark at the end of every other sentence is like writing half your sentences in capitals: if you emphasize everything, you end up emphasizing nothing. Plus it is exhausting (and faintly annoying) to read. Consider this:

> *It was the holiday of a lifetime! We saw eight leopards in six days! Imagine that!! Eight leopards!!!*

If you're a wildlife lover who has been less fortunate with your safari sightings, this over-excitement is just going to irritate you; if you don't know or care if leopards are the ones with stripes or the ones with spots, your indifference is not going to be lessened by exuberant punctuation.

On the other hand, a judiciously used exclamation mark undoubtedly has its place. A famous fashion designer wrote about having spent an hour embroidering a detail on to a gown for a client, without using a thimble:

> *She loved it. But my fingers!*

Lots of people would have written *She loved it!* – but that would have ruined the effect. Here, the exclamation mark is unmistakable shorthand for 'OMG, what a mess my fingers were' and the more powerful for being on its own.

A point of admiration

The exclamation mark used to be called an *admiration mark* or *admiration point*, back in the days when *admiration* meant wonder or astonishment, but not always of a positive kind. In a romantic novel set in the nineteenth century, a young woman receives letters from two relatives who have learned about her unexpected marriage and *sprinkled their letters with points of admiration, obviously agog with curiosity*. Nowadays, those girls would have been messaging their cousin with abbreviations such as OMG or LOL or even with no words at all, just an emoji or three (see page 169).

It's all too common to see exclamation marks used to reinforce a point that doesn't need reinforcing:

Stonehenge was built 5,000 years ago!

Elvis Presley had 56 Top Ten hits!

My response to that would be, 'Actually, I know that Stonehenge is old and that Elvis Presley was successful. Please don't ram it down my throat.' Depending on the circumstances, I might or might not say that out loud.

The same applies to things that simply aren't exclamations:

Roast chicken will be tastier if you leave it to stand before carving!

It's up to you to decide if Ross Poldark is a hero or a villain!

The punctuation here adds nothing; worse, it devalues the exclamation mark for when you really have something to exclaim about.

So when *do* you use it?

Well, for something that justifies it: it's particularly useful in direct speech if you want to indicate emotions such as urgency, anger, dismay or enthusiasm:

Look out! There's a train coming!

What nonsense!

Oh no! That's terrible!

What a beautiful morning!

In all these cases, the exclamation mark gives a clue to the tone in which the words are spoken, and as such gives an insight into the speaker's feelings.

It's my birthday! conveys exuberance; without the exclamation mark, I might be bemoaning the fact that I am another year older.

You're an idiot! expresses annoyance; without the exclamation mark, the words could be a resigned statement of fact. You could convey the same nuance with

'It's my birthday,' she chirped

or

'It's my birthday,' she said despondently.

Likewise:

'You're an idiot,' he snapped

or

'You're an idiot,' he said resignedly.

As so often, it's up to you. The point is to be aware of the effect you are creating – and to ensure that it is the effect you want.

If a literary reviewer writes *I love this book for its subtle evocation of the seedy side of Hollywood life*, the sentence comes across as thoughtful – she's read the book carefully and this is her considered opinion. A less formal review on a web forum might say *I love this book! It shows Hollywood as really seedy!*, suggesting that the author has never previously thought of Hollywood as being seedy (where has she been?). Neither is 'wrong', but the tones are completely different.

The accidental exclamation mark!

There's a chain of estate agents called *Belvoir!* and one at least of its branches uses the slogan *Be! with Belvoir*. Does this sort of thing – and it has taken all the self-control of which I am capable not to type 'this sort of nonsense' – sell more houses? I have no idea. Just round the corner from that particular branch of *Belvoir!* was something called *{my} dentist*. Do these bizarre brackets make sufferers feel better about having their teeth filled? Are the good people of the chilly small town where I spotted this particularly susceptible to the marketing power of punctuation? More research needed – perhaps on a slightly warmer day.

The measured comma and the breathless dash

It isn't just the exclamation mark that conveys emotion. All sorts of punctuation can change the pace or tone of your writing. In particular, commas can make what you have written seem measured or leisurely; dashes speed it up and make it more exciting and breathless.

Compare:

I'm telling you this because, as you do not seem to realize, there are rules in this department

or

Gradually, the noise of the traffic died away, the shadows lengthened and we could look forward to a peaceful evening

with

I didn't know what time it was – didn't know what day it was, really – couldn't believe that this was happening or

> *What I should have said – what I really wanted the courage to say – was that you should get a grip – get a job, even – just get off your backside and do something with your life.*

Re-punctuate those examples, using dashes instead of commas and vice versa, and they'll just look odd.

Dashes and ellipses also show hesitation, nervousness, uncertainty:

> *This isn't ... I don't know how to put it ... I can't do ... It would be wrong.*

Or they show that something has been left unsaid:

> *Other people seem to make their relationships work. Whereas you and I—*
>
> *The two elder boys seem to be settling down at school, but little Sam ...*

They can convey sorrow. The punctuation in

> *Would you mind telling her? I don't think I ...*

suggests that the end of the sentence would have been *could bear to*, and perhaps even that the speaker is close to tears. To add something like *She broke off, emotion choking her* would be heavy-handed, because those three little dots have told you that.

They can show that you are seeking the right word, or don't actually want to put your thoughts into words: *His attitudes are old-fashioned* could be taken at face value; add an ellipsis – *his attitudes are … old-fashioned* – and you have the implication of 'How shall I put this? I don't want to come right out and say that he's a bigot.'

Or, as anyone who has seen *Mamma Mia!* will know, they suggest that something sexual is taking place: *We danced on the beach, and we kissed on the beach, and … dot, dot, dot*, reads young Sophie from her mother's diary; when her friends ask what this means she explains, *Dot, dot, dot. That's what they did in the olden days.* It's a punctuational concept that got a bad name in the heyday of Barbara Cartland, but can still have its place when you don't want to go into X-rated details.

Dashes for emphasis

Not expressing emotion, exactly, but look at this sentence from Donna Leon's *Drawing Conclusions*:

> *Though Brunetti was the son, grandson, great-grandson*
> *– and more – of Venetians, he had always found greater*
> *comfort in the sight of mountains than in that of the sea.*

I quote it because of the dashes, because of the way they make *and more* stand out. Ms Leon could equally well have written

Though Brunetti was the son, grandson, great-grandson and more of Venetians . . .

but by putting those two words between dashes she draws attention to them, suggesting that Brunetti's Venetian heritage goes back not just four or five generations but into the mists of time. It's subtle, but it's there if you want to look for it.

●

Italics for emphasis

If you wrote, without particular emphasis, *I've just done a load of washing*, most people would assume that you had filled and emptied the washing machine once and once only – a *load* being a measure of quantity on a par with a bucket of water or a bottle of lemonade.

But *I've just done a* load *of washing* suggests you've been at it all day, filling the machine over and over again and clearing a considerable backlog. Emphasizing the word puts what you have been doing on a par with *a load of ironing* or a teacher doing *a load of marking*, where a *load* means a great deal, not just the amount you put into one washing machine.

You can also use italics to emphasize part of a quotation, in which case you'd note that fact in square brackets (see page 52):

The great sociobiologist E. O. Wilson wrote of Marxism that, although it was 'formulated as the enemy of ignorance and

superstition [my emphasis], to the extent that it has become
dogmatic it has faltered in that commitment'.

This tells us that Professor Wilson didn't particularly emphasize the words *formulated as the enemy of ignorance and superstition*, but that the writer who is quoting them wants to draw them to our attention – they are helping to make his point.

Unless you are a skilled calligrapher, you probably don't distinguish between italics and normal (roman) characters when writing by hand; in that case, underlining serves the same purpose.

Some italic conventions

Italics are generally used for the titles of books, newspapers, magazines, plays, films, musical compositions and the names of ships:

- *Harry Potter and the Chamber of Secrets*
- *National Enquirer*
- *Death of a Salesman*
- *My Life as a Zucchini*
- Beethoven's *Moonlight Sonata*
- RMS *Lusitania*

An odd exception is that we don't use italics for the names of sacred texts: it's the Bible, the Talmud, the Qur'an and, while we are at it, the Old Testament, the New Testament, Genesis, Exodus, Matthew, Mark, Luke and John.

$\longrightarrow$

Italics are used for foreign words and can be useful for highlighting technical terms (though, again, if your main statement happens to be printed in italic, as my examples are, you of course need to reverse the process and use roman for emphasis and highlighting):

> *The choir sang beautifully, particularly in the* a cappella *anthem.*

> *He is always full of* joie de vivre.

> *Use a comma before what is known as a* question tag.

Once a foreign expression has become well established in English, the need to use italics drifts away, like the need for hyphens discussed earlier (page 65). This is perhaps a matter of taste and judgement, but I'd be inclined to think it was old-fashioned and/or pretentious to italicize *furore*, *peccadillo*, *mantra* or *robot*, despite their undoubted foreign origins.

In the natural world, names of species and genera are, by convention, written in italics, but larger groupings are not: thus *Quercus robur* (the English oak) is a species of the *Quercus* genus, which is a subdivision of the Fagaceae family; *Panthera leo* (the lion) belongs to the *Panthera* genus, the family Felidae and the order Carnivora.

And finally, court cases – should you have occasion to refer to them – also go in italics, as in *R.* versus *Penguin Books Ltd* (the 'Lady Chatterley' trial).

Capitals for emphasis

Newspapers and magazines often print the first word or two of an article in capital letters, omitting any punctuation that would have been used had these words appeared later on. As readers, we're used to this, but it was unfortunate in one piece I spotted recently. The actor's name was given, but isn't relevant here, which is why I've replaced it with Xs.

> SHAMELESS actor XXXX has been cleared of [a charge brought against him].

At first glance, this might have seemed like a disparaging journalistic comment on the man concerned. But no. The actor used to appear in the television comedy *Shameless*, as the use of italics or inverted commas would have made clear.

●

Punctuation for comic effect

For comic effect? Really? Oh yes.

If you know the mock-historians Sellar and Yeatman's comic masterpiece *1066 and All That*, you'll know what magic can be worked with capital letters. (If you don't know it, do seek it out. It was first published in 1930 and is still hilarious.) The book has the sprawling subtitle *A Memorable History of England comprising all the parts you can remember including 103 Good Things, 5 Bad Kings and 2 Genuine Dates* and throughout the text the authors capitalize not only *Good Thing* but *Good King, Bad King,*

Olden Days and much more. It's very much in keeping with the tone of the book, which also refers to Alfred the Cake and Queen Victoria's Jamboree and maintains that King Arthur was married to Lady Windermere.

For those who haven't read it, by the way, the second date covered is 55 BC, Julius Caesar's invasion of Britain. Whether or not that would now come under the heading of 'as every schoolchild knows' is a discussion for another day.

I came across a similar jokey use of capitals in an article about scaremongering journalism: *Bird flu is going to Invade Our Country and Kill Us All.* The author could have written *bird flu is going to invade our country and kill us all,* if she had intended it as a statement of fact; or she could have used distance quotes (*'is going to invade our country and kill us all'* – see page 146) to separate herself from what had been said by others. But the out-of-place capitals draw scathing attention to the shock-horror nature of the original reports.

Funnily enough, that author could have achieved much the same effect with hyphens, had she chosen, for example, to refer to the *bird-flu-is-going-to-invade-our-country-and-kill-us-all school of journalism.*

Then there is capitalization-to-denote-pomposity: in Georgette Heyer's Regency novel *The Grand Sophy*, a nobleman's children having allowed their pet monkey to escape from the nursery, the butler lets it be known that *Wild Animals roaming at large in a Nobleman's Residence were not what he had been accustomed to.* Writing in the mid-twentieth century, Heyer was perhaps mimicking the style of the period she was evoking (see the reference to *Golden Hill* on page 26), some hundred and fifty years earlier, but those mid-sentence capitals serve as a mini character sketch of a man more concerned with his own dignity than with any havoc the monkey might cause.

An article about the restaurant industry referred to *the world of Chef-as-proper-noun … a narrative of the infallible chef, ruthless in the pursuit of 'perfection'*. Giving the name an initial capital certainly elevates the status of the mere chef – he or she ceases to be one up from a common-or-garden cook and becomes a high-achieving seeker after celebrity status, probably terrorizing a kitchenful of hapless underlings. Note also the use of distance or scare quotes (see page 146): putting inverted commas round *perfection* turns it into shorthand for 'what some people think of as perfection but I frankly do not'.

●

For a laugh, ha ha ha …

Capitals are one thing; imagine using ellipses for comic effect.

Consider this piece of dialogue from novelist and playwright Michael Frayn's *The Russian Interpreter*. One of the speakers has stolen the other man's girlfriend and is trying to apologize for being 'rather a bastard'; the other wants to reassure him:

'Honestly, Gordon, there's no need to feel ...'

   'I mean, I know all's fair in love and war ...'

'Gordon, there's really no need to feel, you know ...'

   'You mean, you don't feel, well ...?'

'Of course not, Gordon. I mean, there's no need to feel, you know ...'

   'Really? Well, I appreciate that, Paul. It shows a generous spirit, and I appreciate it.'

It's not that Gordon and Paul are interrupting each other; instead, their voices are trailing away at the end of each sentence. Take away the dots and you have a banal exchange; with them, you have a witty piece of dialogue between two archetypically inarticulate English males struggling to express their feelings.

Points of style

There's no real difference between a dash and an ellipsis in the above context: choose the one you prefer and stick to it. At the end of a sentence ending in an ellipsis, some people add a full stop, giving four dots in all (....), but many people (by which I suppose I mean many publishers) now consider this old-fashioned and don't bother.

   I was recently reading an Agatha Christie novel in an old edition picked up in a second-hand shop. It's full of dialogue in which the speaker hesitates or interrupts himself: *'I have come across certain things which are, I may say—very curious—very—how shall I put it?—suggestive?'* That sort of thing. Mrs Christie, or her (British) publisher, chose to use closed-up em (–) dashes throughout. And at one point the police superintendent is describing the suspect:

> *'Thirty-three, medium height, sallow complexion, wears glasses——'*

Poirot interrupts – he's interested in the man's personality, not his looks. And the end of the interrupted sentence is marked not by one em dash but by two.

This was obviously acceptable typography in the 1950s; a 1980s reissue of the same book from a new incarnation of the same publisher used the more modern spaced en dashes throughout (*very – how shall I put it? – suggestive*), with only a single spaced en dash at the end of the superintendent's speech. And another author could have chosen, as Michael Frayn did in the example above, to use ellipses instead.

Dash it

This is a matter of usage more than of punctuation, but worth a brief mention because it is frequently seen and (IMHO) sloppy.

If you are expressing a range of numbers or dates, you have

two options: the range is either *from* something *to* something else, or it is *between* one thing *and* another:

Terry Pratchett lived from 1948 to 2015. He published most of his novels between 1983 and 2004.

In formal writing, this is what you would put. If you wanted to reduce the information to a biographical note, you could go for:

Terry Pratchett lived 1948–2015. Published most of his novels 1983–2004.

The punctuation mark you are using here is a dash, not a hyphen. But that is less important than the fact that you should never write

He lived from 1948–2015.

He published most of his novels between 1983–2004.

The moment you introduce the dash, you need to get rid of the words *from* and *between*. The moment you use those words, you get rid of the dash. Formal is fine; informal, note-style is fine in context. A mishmash of the two is just messy.

7

Things That May Confuse: I

Apostrophe ('): *the punctuation mark used to form the possessive, as in* Charlie's Angels *and/or to indicate the omission of a letter or a number, as in the* Swingin' '60s.

There's been so much fuss about apostrophes in recent years that some people have called for them to be abolished altogether. This upsets me, not because I am easily upset nor because I am ridiculously pernickety (though both of these things may be true), but because I genuinely don't believe that apostrophes are as difficult to master as all that.

But there is no denying that they are very frequently misused. A friend who breeds dogs sometimes receives communications enquiring about *a litter of puppy's*. 'A litter of puppy's what?' she is tempted to ask. 'A litter of puppy's

diet? A litter of puppy's housetraining? It makes no sense.'
She also notes that people who have bought a single puppy
from her can be accurate about, say, *the puppy's feeding
time*; those who've bought two are more likely to write *the
puppies feeding time* with no apostrophe at all.

To be fair, a number of her correspondents are not
native English speakers; none of them, so far as she knows,
is a journalist or publisher. More reprehensible, therefore,
to my mind, is the newspaper report of an industrial
dispute in a major publishing house, which quoted a
management spokesperson as saying that there was *no
change to individual employee's terms and conditions*. True,
the publisher may have been making a verbal statement,
in which case it would be the journalists reporting it who
should be ashamed of themselves. But whoever is to
blame, it seems a shame that only one employee (out of
many hundreds) should be reassured.

Industrial disputes seem prone to poor apostrophizing;
another piece at around the same time wrote about a
demand to *increase nurses and doctors pay*. On the face of
it, and in the absence of apostrophes, this is proposing to
increase (the number of) nurses, for which doctors will foot
the bill – an attractive but unlikely proposition, most nurses
would suggest. Or it could be warning that if you increase
the number of nurses, doctors will pay – whether financially
or in some other way isn't specified. What it should say is
increase nurses' and doctors' pay – in other words, improve
the salaries of both groups (another unlikely proposition

and one which some nurses might suggest).

If all this means nothing to you, it may be time for me to stop being facetious and to start trying to explain.

Possession, association and the like

One of the two principal uses of apostrophes is to indicate possession, association and other related qualities. The rules are:

- If the person or thing doing the possessing is singular, or if you are dealing with a plural not ending in *s* (*children*, *geese*, etc. – see below), follow it with an apostrophe and an *s*.
- If they are plural, and that plural ends in *s*, simply add an apostrophe.

So, to go back to the examples given a moment ago, we have:

the puppy's feeding time (one puppy) but *the puppies' feeding time* (two or more of them).

individual employees' terms and conditions (all of them); an *individual employee's terms and conditions* would refer to one employee only.

nurses' and doctors' pay (again referring to all of them). If you were a small establishment that employed only one nurse and one doctor, you would refer to *the nurse's and the doctor's pay*, using the definite article and positioning the apostrophes like this.

most English plurals do end in *s*, though some of them achieve this by adding *-es* to the singular noun (*churches*, *foxes*, *waltzes*) and some by changing a *y* to an *i* and adding *-es* (*puppy/puppies*, *candy/candies*, *tally/tallies*). Words that have an *f* at or near the end sometimes change this to a *v* (*wife/wives*, *hoof/hooves*) and there is also a handful of words that end in *-is* in the singular and *-es* in the plural (*analysis/analyses*, *crisis/crises* and, most relevantly for this book, *ellipsis/ellipses*). But the rule remains the same – if the plural ends in *s*, add an apostrophe and nothing else: *the foxes' den*, *the candies' sweetness*, *the hooves' drumming*, *the crises' aftermaths*.

Then there are the plurals that don't end in *s*, because either they are irregular forms taken from Old English (*children*, *geese*, *mice*, *teeth*); or they come from Latin or Greek and use the form they would have had in those languages (*cacti*, *formulae*, *phenomena*); or the singular is the same as the plural (*aircraft*, *deer*, *sheep*). For the purposes of possessive apostrophes (but not for any other purpose, grammatical or otherwise), treat these as if they were singular and add *apostrophe + s*:

the children's toys, the cacti's prickles, the deer's antlers.

If you need to clarify your thoughts, rephrase in your head before you write anything down:

The feeding time of the [single] *puppy? Puppy + 's = the puppy's feeding time*

The feeding time of the [several] *puppies? Puppies + ' = the puppies' feeding time*

The [only] *nurse's uniform? Nurse + 's = the nurse's uniform*

The salaries of [a vast number of] *nurses? Nurses + ' = the nurses' salaries*

The toys of the children? Children + 's = the children's toys.

The den of the [lonesome] *fox? The fox + 's = the fox's den*

The den of the [family of] *foxes? The foxes + ' = the foxes' den*

The wool of the [unspecified number from one upwards] *sheep? The sheep + 's = the sheep's wool*

... and so on.

How many goats make cheese?

You could take issue with the logic of this, but convention has it that *goat's cheese* is spelled thus, as if it were the cheese made from (the milk of) a single goat. Similarly *lamb's wool* and various plants whose folk names liken them to parts of an animal, such as *lamb's ears* and *goat's beard*. Also, bizarrely, *collector's item*, though the allegedly acquisitive nature of collectors means that, even if an item belongs to only one of them at once, it can be coveted by many.

●

Names ending in s

Opinions vary over what to do with these. In England alone there are three different ways of spelling a park associated with St James: it can be *St James*, *St James'* or *St James's*. The first is obviously pronounced *James*, the last *Jameses*, but with the one in the middle you can take your pick. (If you find this confusing, let me urge you to avoid the Wikipedia page about the Newcastle United football ground, which happens to be St James' Park – it won't make your life any easier.)

Let's try for a few guidelines. Names ending in *s* are generally followed by *'s*:

Bridget Jones's Diary

Charles Dickens's novels

Cassius's lean and hungry look

and the *s* is pronounced, so that these examples would sound like *Joneses*, *Dickenses* and *Cassiuses*.

But all of these are fairly easy to say. Once you're faced with something more tongue-twisting, forget about that additional *s*, just add an apostrophe and pronounce it as you would pronounce the name on its own:

> *Archimedes' principle*
>
> *Sophocles' dramas*
>
> *Mephistopheles' evilness*

The moment you start to feel you are tying yourself in knots, rephrase:

> *The principle of Archimedes*
>
> *The dramas of Sophocles*
>
> *The evilness of Mephistopheles*

Not only does it sound better, it means you can forget about the apostrophes altogether.

Here is a howler, from the caption (in yet another art gallery) to a portrait of the artist Peter Lely: *The confident stance and fashionable dress reflect Lely's grand way of living, as the diarist Samuel Pepys's noted, calling him 'a mighty proud man, and full of state'. Lely's* is perfectly correct; what that *'s* is doing tacked on to the end of *Pepys* is anybody's guess.

The 'covering my back' apostrophe

That Pepys example (see main text) shows a common error among those who are unconfident about apostrophes.

Worried about being despised for leaving them out, they introduce them where they have no business to be. To give another instance:

Varying the alcohol levels [at a wine tasting] *gives the palates of your guests' time to attune . . .*

The writer has clearly become confused between what he has written and *your guests' palates*, which would have been correct, indicating that the palates belonged to the guests. But in the construction he has chosen, as in the ones to do with Archimedes and Mephistopheles (see main text), the apostrophe has no function. Leave it out.

Spell it the way they spell it

Brand names from Harrods to McDonald's, and place names from King's Cross in London to Kings Cross in Sydney, make their own rules. The only answer is to check websites, maps and carrier bags, as appropriate, and do what they do. If you attempt to apply logic, as with the St James's example above, you'll end up tearing out a lot of hair.

And it's not just apostrophes: many, many companies use deliberate misspellings, non-standard capitalization and weird diacritic marks (accents and the like, see page 157) to give themselves a trademark they can register, or just to catch the public eye. Perhaps the most noticeable, because it happened in 1948, long before this sort of thing was commonplace, is Toys "Я" Us with its odd punctuation and reversed R; the company's founder Charles Lazarus is quoted as having ignored the parents and teachers who objected to its grammatical incorrectness because he 'knew it was an attention-getter'. He seems to have been right: the company now has over 1,500 outlets worldwide.

But motivation needn't concern us here. What does concern us is that, from Dunkin' Donuts and Gü to WhatsApp and Flickr, the spelling and punctuation these companies have chosen are 'correct' as far as their brands are concerned. However wrong they may be really.

What's mine is yours . . .

If you are naming two people who own or are associated with the same thing, put an apostrophe + *s* only after the second:

Will and Kate's baby (not *Will's and Kate's*)

George and Amal's home

Brad and Angelina's separation

On the other hand, put an apostrophe after the first name in expressions such as

Andy's and my office (the office I share with Andy)

The professor's and your research (the research you and the professor are doing)

Tim's and her engagement (the engagement between Tim and a female you've mentioned already)

●

. . . but you don't have to say so

The thing being possessed doesn't need to be specified for an apostrophe to be necessary. Look at:

My uncle's land adjoined my parents'.

He was less comfortable with his own emotions than with others'.

Plymouth has been the starting point for many famous voyages, including Sir Francis Drake's and the Pilgrim Fathers'.

In sentences such as these, we understand that we're talking about *my parents' land*, *others' emotions* and *Drake and the Pilgrim Fathers' voyages*. If we chose to rephrase, we could do away with the apostrophes:

My uncle's land adjoined that of my parents.

He was less comfortable with his own emotions than with those of others.

Plymouth has been the starting point for many famous voyages, including those of Sir Francis Drake and the Pilgrim Fathers.

In this context, *those of* and *that of* replace the implicit *land*, *emotions* and *voyages* of the original phrasing. It's the same concept as replacing *Mephistopheles' evilness* with *the evilness of Mephistopheles*, as mentioned earlier.

Something's missing

The second principal use of an apostrophe is to show that a letter or letters have been left out. The most common examples occur in words such as *won't*, *can't*, *didn't* and *haven't*, where the apostrophe indicates the missing *o* of *not*; and *I've*, *you're*, *she's*, *we'd* and *they'll* which are abbreviated forms of *I have*, *you are*, *she is*, *we had* (or *we would/should*) and *they will*.

I won't be long.

You can't be serious.

He isn't coming.

We weren't there; we don't know anything about it.

They wouldn't have done something like that.

I've never been to New York.

You're only twelve – you're too young to see that film.

She's been gone a long time.

We're playing tennis on Saturday.

They're only after her money.

It's (or it is, see below) worth pointing out that these are all informal – when making a date with a friend it's fine to say *I'll see you tomorrow*; if it's a business arrangement, *I shall look forward to our meeting* is probably more appropriate.

You may observe that *won't*, *shan't* and *can't* are short for *will not*, *shall not* and *cannot*, all of which are missing more letters than the *o* of *not*. That's true, but it's also one of those things you just have to put up with: *won't*, *shan't* and *can't* are the standard, accepted spellings.

Over the centuries we have, for some reason, retained the apostrophe in a handful of words such as *o'clock* (which was once short for *of the clock*) and *Hallowe'en* (where the last part is short for *even*, itself an archaic word for *eve* or *evening*); in poetic or archaic forms such as *o'er* for *over* and *'twas* for *it was*; and in colloquial expressions such as *'fraid so* for *I'm afraid so*. But some dictionaries now give *Halloween* as an acceptable alternative; if you were reproducing a conversation in a deliberately slangy style you might dispense with the apostrophe in *fraid*; and it can only be a matter of time before *oclock* goes the same way. For more on this 'times change and we must change with them – or must we?' theme, see the section on clipped forms on page 154.

In dates, what is missing might be a number, as in *the 1940s and '50s*, *the '45 Rebellion* or *the class of '98*.

There is no need to put an apostrophe before the *s* that follows an abbreviation, if what you are doing is making a plural:

The MPs were unanimous in their approval.

But you do need it if you are indicating possession or association:

The MPs' vote was unanimous.

Similarly

My CDs are arranged in chronological order

but

My CDs' covers faded when I left them in the sun.

And I've just read an advertisement for a film *set in 1940's London*. No, no, no. There is no need for an apostrophe here: *1940s* counts as an adjective, on a par with *wartime London* or *bomb-damaged London*. If you felt that logically there was an element of 'association or possession', it would still need to be *1940s' London* – the London of the 1940s. As it stands, *1940's London* suggests that the film ends before 1 January 1941. It doesn't. I've seen it.

Sometimes it just feels right

I expect you'll agree that *minding your ps and qs, dotting your is* and *crossing your ts* all look a bit odd. There's no logical, grammatical reason to write *p's and q's* or *i's and t's* - or, indeed, *do's and don'ts* - but most writers do simply because they look clearer and making things look clearer is one of the things that punctuation is all about.

Personally speaking

Here's a rule: the personal pronouns *yours*, *its*, *his*, *hers*, *ours* and *theirs* don't have apostrophes:

My hands are smaller than yours.

I hate my flat – I'd much rather live in his.

Your dress is beautiful, but hers *is even lovelier.*

Your holiday sounds much more fun than ours.

Theirs *is the most expensive car in the village.*

Its doesn't crop up often as a personal pronoun, but you might find it in (rather contrived) sentences such as

That isn't my dog's collar – its *is the blue one over there.*

More frequently, you come across *its* as a determiner meaning 'belonging to or in some way associated with it':

The dog hates having its *collar put on.*

The car had a long scratch down its *right-hand side.*

I've read that book so often that its *pages are falling out.*

This sort of *its* doesn't have an apostrophe either, and putting one in is probably the most common punctuation mistake of all. In fact, the only time that *it's* is correct is when it is short for *it is* or *it has*:

Your dinner is in the oven: it's *probably burned by now.*

It's *a long story – are you sitting comfortably?*

The car looks as if it's *been in an accident.*

It's *been a long time since we met.*

It's worth recapitulating, because this is probably the firmest rule in this book: if you can't expand *it's* to mean *it is* or *it has*, don't use an apostrophe.

There is also no such word as *its'*. If there were, it would refer to something that belonged to *its*, which makes no sense at all.

One of those things

When *one* is used as an indefinite pronoun, it forms a possessive with an apostrophe + s:

One has to mind one's *language in front of her.*

One ought always to wash one's *hands before meals.*

Don't ask. It just does.

Some confusables

English is full of homophones – words that sound alike but are usually spelled differently and often have completely unrelated meanings. Think of the difference between *bear* (the animal, or a verb meaning to tolerate) and *bare* (naked, unadorned); *peel* (the outside of an orange) and *peal* (the sound a bell makes); or *right* (correct or the opposite of left), *write* (put pen to paper) and *rite* (a formal act or ceremony).

This potential source of confusion can involve apostrophes, too. You should be aware of the difference between:

Their *attitude is deplorable* (the attitude associated with *them*)

There *is a world of difference between them* (with *there* representing the indefinite subject of a sentence)

I left my coat over there (*in that position,* further away than *here*)

They're *in here somewhere* (short for *they are,* hence the apostrophe)

Whose *are those boots?* (in other words, *to whom do those boots belong?*)

The candidate whose *credentials had looked so impressive turned out to be completely hopeless* (the credentials belonging to that candidate)

Who's *afraid of the big bad wolf?* (short for *who is,* hence the apostrophe)

Who's *been sleeping in my bed?* (short for *who has,* ditto)

Your *coat is far too big for you* (the coat belonging to you)

You're *always taking on too much work* (short for *you are*, hence the apostrophe)

This last example means that *Christmas starts early when your an Interior Designer!* – which I noticed in an August issue of a magazine – is wrong on all sorts of levels. There's the grandiose use of capitals for *Interior Designer* (see my remarks on Chefs on page 108); there's the what-the-devil-is-there-to-exclaim-about? use of an exclamation mark (see page 97); there's the just-plain-wrong use of *your*; and there's the hideous concept of talking about Christmas in August.

●

Could of been a contender

This isn't the place – or the book – to go into great detail about auxiliary verbs, but they deserve a passing mention because of their role in the 'misuse of apostrophes' debacle.

An auxiliary verb is one that is used to indicate the tense, mood or voice of another verb.

He will be *travelling a lot this year* (*will be* puts the action in the future tense).

They have *gone to New Zealand* (*have* puts it in the past tense).

You should have *been here earlier* (*should have* gives a past conditional, indicating something that didn't happen).

If it were *to stop raining, we could go out* (*were* indicates the subjunctive mood, showing that we don't know if it is going to stop raining or not).

It has been *said that punctuation is difficult* (*has been* is the passive voice, where the person who said this is not specified).

And we care about this in a book on punctuation because ..?

Well, the only bits of this that concern us here are the examples containing *have*. Here are some more:

By the end of this week I will have *been here for two years.*

We would have *come if you had invited us sooner.*

And Marlon Brando's famous reproach to his brother in *On the Waterfront*:

I could have *been a contender.*

In speech and in informal writing, these verbs are often abbreviated to *will've*, *would've*, *could've*, with the apostrophe indicating that the *ha* of *have* has been omitted. The problem is that *will've* sounds very like *will of*, *would've* like *would of* and so on. But grammatically speaking, *will of*, *would of* etc. make no sense. *Of* is a preposition, conveying a wide range of associations from *the Seven Wonders of the World* to *the many moons of Jupiter*, *the drop of a hat* to *the tip of the iceberg*. But it is never, ever part of an auxiliary verb. If you come across *would've*, *could've* etc. and think they are too informal for your context, spell them out as *would have* or *could have*. And if you think you've heard people saying *would of*, *could of* etc., you may well have done – just don't write them down that way.

Orange's and lemon's: the accidental apostrophe's

One place you don't – you really don't – need an apostrophe is where you are forming the plural of a word that happens to end in a vowel: the all-too-commonly seen *satsuma's*, *tomato's*, *potato's* and so on are wrong unless they come in contexts such as *that satsuma's got lots of pips in it*, *a tomato's skin will come off easily if you plunge it into boiling water* or *the potato's jacket was wonderfully crispy*. The out-of-place apostrophe in plurals has become so common on fruit and veg stalls that I was cheered, wandering through a market recently, to see a sign advertising what I thought were apostrophe-free *bananas*. My cheer didn't last long: a second glance showed that that particular stallholder was offering *banananas*. Never mind, I thought, at least he hasn't got the apostrophe wrong. Then I noticed that his neighbour, going one better, had a special price for *bananana's*.

~

8

Things That May Confuse: II

Direct speech: *reporting what someone has said or written by quoting the actual words.*

Indirect or reported speech: *conveying what was meant without giving the exact words.*

Punctuationally speaking, there is a straightforward rule here: if you are quoting someone's words, put them in inverted commas (also known as quotation marks); if you are reporting what they said, don't.

'I really don't know what you're talking about,' she said.

She said she really didn't know what I was talking about.

'I'd love to go to New Zealand,' he moaned.

He moaned that he would love to go to New Zealand.

●

Go directly . . .

Let's concentrate on direct speech for the moment. If you are quoting a statement such as those given above (as opposed to an exclamation or a question), begin with a capital and put a comma *immediately after the words quoted and before the closing inverted comma*. Then, if you have reached the end of a sentence, put a full stop after *she said* or its equivalent, as I have done in the above examples.

If you haven't reached the end of a sentence and the speech continues, *don't put a full stop*, put another comma and continue the speech with a lower-case (small) letter:

'I really don't know what you're talking about,' she said, 'and what's more I don't want to know.'

'I'd love to go to New Zealand,' he growled, 'but I'm never going to be able to afford it.'

This makes sense if you consider the words spoken:

'I really don't know what you're talking about, and what's more I don't want to know.'

'I'd love to go to New Zealand, but I'm never going to be able to afford it.'

Single sentences, so no full stop in the middle. But if the speech you are quoting is two sentences or more:

> 'I really don't know what you're talking about,' she said. 'You always talk such nonsense'

the actual words spoken are:

> 'I really don't know what you're talking about. You always talk such nonsense.'

Two sentences, separated by a full stop, which is followed by a capital letter.

●

She said it first

If *she said* or equivalent comes immediately *before* the quoted words, put a comma after it:

> She said, 'I really don't know what you're talking about.'
>
> He muttered under his breath, 'I'm going to get you for this.'

Before a longer quote, you sometimes see a colon instead of a comma. Here's a piece from Philippa Gregory's *The Other Queen*, about Mary, Queen of Scots:

> Bothwell put his heavy hands on my shoulders and said: 'Marie, listen, your body is not sacred. If it ever was – it is not

sacred any more. I have had it. They all know that I had you,
and without your consent . . .'

There is a lot more in this rather unpleasant vein – Bothwell keeps talking about the ignominious things that have happened and may yet happen to Mary (including having her head cut off) for a full ten lines. You probably won't have a very high opinion of him at the end of the speech, but it's difficult to object to the use of a colon at the start of it.

Bill Bryson did the same thing in *At Home*, quoting an eighteenth-century novelist:

Writing of country life in 1768, Fanny Burney noted: 'We
breakfast always at ten, and rise as much before as we
please; we dine precisely at two, drink tea about six and sup
exactly at nine.'

This is very much a matter of style: a comma after *noted* would not have been wrong, or even unusual, but the colon is fine, too. Having chosen your style, however, stick to it – don't use a comma in one paragraph and a colon in the next. And, in passing, I draw your attention to Ms Burney's immaculate use of a semicolon.

If you are writing a long piece of dialogue or quoting a passage that involves more than one paragraph, put inverted commas at the start of each new paragraph. This helps your reader to understand that what follows is part of the same quotation. But don't put inverted commas at the *end* of each paragraph. Close the inverted commas only at the end of the *final* paragraph, when the speech or quotation is over.

Perverted commas

This term is a coinage of James Joyce, who didn't like inverted commas and instead used an em dash (–) at the start of each new piece of dialogue. Lots of French writers do the same. The disadvantage of this, to my mind, is that it isn't usual to put another dash at the end, so you can't see at a glance where the spoken words end and the narrative continues.

The French also use *guillemets* – « to open inverted commas and » to close them – but these are just different symbols serving the same purpose as '......' or "......".

To ditch them altogether, as James Kelman did (see page 21), seems to me not perverted but perverse. Consider

The police said the accused had thrown the first punch

and

'The police,' said the accused, 'had thrown the first punch.'

Not the same thing at all, I'm sure you'll agree.

Asking a direct question

If you are quoting an exclamation or a question, put the exclamation mark or question mark in the comma's place:

'What are you up to?' Mum asked.

'Stop that at once!' she screamed.

Then, bear in mind that – like full stops – exclamation marks and question marks come at the end of a sentence and are followed by a capital letter. So if you are quoting more words, punctuate them like this:

'What are you up to?' Mum asked. 'You've been very quiet for a long time.'

'Stop that at once!' she screamed. 'How many times do I have to tell you?'

Again, look at the actual words:

'What are you up to? You've been very quiet for a long time.'

'Stop that at once! How many times do I have to tell you?'

… and, with any luck, the logic becomes clear.
Here's another set of examples:

'There's no food in the house,' Sam growled, 'and I'm starving.'

'There's no food in the house,' Sam growled. 'Why haven't you done the shopping?'

'Why haven't you done the shopping?' Sam growled. 'There's no food in the house.'

'I'm starving!' Sam shouted. 'Why isn't there any food in the house?'

Again, look at the words spoken in each case to help you work out where full stops and capital letters should go:

'There's no food in the house, and I'm starving.'

'There's no food in the house. Why haven't you done the shopping?'

'Why haven't you done the shopping? There's no food in the house.'

'I'm starving! Why isn't there any food in the house?'

But note one variation that never happens: *'There's no food in the house.' growled Sam*, with a full stop before the inverted comma, is wrong.

Remember, also (see page 18), that it is conventional to give each new speaker a new paragraph:

'There's no food in the house,' Sam growled. 'Why haven't you done the shopping?'

'Why haven't you done the shopping, come to that?' Alex retorted. 'Why should I run around after you all the time?'

'You don't understand how tired I get!' Sam shouted from halfway up the stairs. 'I simply don't have the energy.'

From this layout it is clear that Sam is asking why Alex hasn't done the shopping. If, instead, I had written:

'There's no food in the house,' moaned Sam.
'Why haven't you done the shopping?'

the fact that I had put the second sentence on a new line would indicate that an unnamed new speaker was asking Sam that question.

Double or single?

Most British publishers and newspapers prefer 'single quotes'. If need be, they then use "double quotes" to distinguish a quote-within-a-quote (see main text). American style tends to be the other way round. It doesn't matter which you go for, as long as you are consistent.

Quotes within quotes

Punctuation is a little more complicated if you are quoting words that include a quote from someone else:

'I'm going to recite some Shakespeare,' Ellie said. '"All the world's a stage …" and stuff like that.'

Jon was reading the newspaper. 'According to this, "fares are going up in line with inflation" and the rail company is "striving to provide the level of service our customers deserve". What garbage.'

In the first example, the double quotes round *All the world's a stage* indicate that these are Shakespeare's words, not Ellie's. In the second, *fares are going up in line with inflation* and *striving to provide the level of service our customers deserve* are words that Jon is quoting from the paper. Grammatically, the quoted words *striving to provide the level of service our customers deserve* end before the end of the sentence, so the closing quotation marks come *before* the full stop.

A book I read about the stresses of modern life contained the question *How often, when someone asks, 'How are you?', have you replied, 'Really busy'?* You may think that that last question mark is misplaced, but look again. The first quotation – *How are you?* – is a question, ending in a question mark. The response – *Really busy* – isn't a question. It's the whole sentence (beginning *How often* …) that is a question. So the quoted words *really busy* sit between quotation marks and are followed by the question mark that ends the sentence.

Don't panic. This won't come up very often.

●

Don't quote me

All that business about putting a comma before the inverted comma presupposes that you are using an expression such as *he said*. But you *can* quote direct speech without doing that, and in that case you don't need that comma. Look at this example from Katie Fforde's *Artistic Licence*:

'I don't mind work.' Susan gave the word emphasis to make clear it was Thea she objected to, not a bit of extra washing up. 'I did do the dishes from last night.' Thea sounded like Petal trying to placate her landlady.

There you have two pieces of direct speech – *I don't mind work* and *I did do the dishes from last night* – written in such a way that the words *Susan said* or *Thea said* would have been superfluous. So the speeches simply come to an end (and require a full stop) before the closing quotation marks. If Katie had chosen to write

'I don't mind work,' *Susan said, giving the word emphasis . . .*

she would have punctuated it like that.

I think it's direct speech

There's a slightly illogical convention that if you are quoting a person's thoughts, rather than anything they have said out loud, you don't use inverted commas – even though you are using their exact words. Thus:

'I wonder what that's doing there,' she said

but

I wonder what that's doing there, she thought.

It wouldn't be wrong to use inverted commas for the thought – just don't be surprised if you find that a lot of writers don't.

Indirect speech

There are a few pointers that will help you get this right. First, remember that you are not quoting exact words (however close to the original you may be) and therefore you don't need quotation marks:

> *'I'm going to be late home.'*
> *She warned me (that) she was going to be late home.*
>
> *'You'd better hurry or you'll miss the train.'*
> *He told me (that) I had better hurry or I would miss the train.*
>
> *'Tell the manager you have a doctor's appointment on Friday.'*
> *She reminded me to tell the manager (that) I had a doctor's appointment on Friday.*

Second, something that was spoken as a question or an exclamation becomes a mere statement when it is reported.

'What are we waiting for?' is a question and therefore has a question mark at the end of it.

She asked what we were waiting for is a statement and, if it came at the end of a sentence, would take simply a full stop.

'Help me, somebody!' he yelled sounds desperate enough to merit an exclamation mark.

He yelled for somebody to help him is, again, reporting something that loses its excitement in the telling and needs only a full stop.

Similarly,

'Is this a dagger which I see before me?' but *He wondered if that was a dagger which he saw before him.*

'My kingdom for a horse!' but *He offered his kingdom for a horse.*

'It's an emergency!' but *He screamed that it was an emergency.*

'Who wants to be a millionaire?' but *He asked who wanted to be a millionaire.*

What's past is past

A final pointer about indirect speech: according to a rule called the sequence of tenses, the tense of the verb in the subordinate clause should match the tense of the main verb.

Eh?

OK. Look at the difference between:

Shakespeare wrote *that all the world* was *a stage*

Shakespeare writes *that all the world* is *a stage.*

The first has two past tenses, the second two present tenses.

Similarly:

'It's awfully hot in here'

could be reported as either

She said that it was awfully hot in here

or, to give more immediacy (perhaps Granny hasn't heard and wants the words to be repeated),

She says that it is awfully hot in here.

Again, either two past tenses or two present ones.

A statement made in a future tense is reported in a conditional. For example:

'I shall come tomorrow'

becomes

She said she would come tomorrow.

Something already in the past has to go further into the past (the past perfect or pluperfect tense), usually formed with *had*:

'He arrived two days ago'

becomes

She said he had arrived two days ago.

I realize that this is not strictly speaking to do with punctuation, but it may enable you to recognize indirect speech when you see it and therefore help you to punctuate it.

Distance quotes

You know that annoying habit some people have of making quotation marks in the air with their fingers, often saying, 'Quote' as they do so? It indicates that other people have called this thing by this name; the speaker is simply repeating what has been said, not endorsing it.

Well, if you do want to do that in writing, you use quotation marks – what are sometimes called 'distance quotes' or 'scare quotes'. You might have used them in the UK to refer to the 'dodgy dossier' involved in the 2003 invasion of Iraq or more recently in the US when discussing 'Cablegate', the leaking of classified cables sent to the Department of State. Or you could do it when using a nickname for a celebrity or a famous event – the (quote) 'Boston Strangler' or the (so-called) 'Rumble in the Jungle'. By putting these terms in quotation marks you are distancing yourself from them, acknowledging that you haven't invented them and that they don't necessarily reflect your own views.

Then, as terms like this become familiar and accepted, the need for the quotes disappears. I doubt if many people today would put Scary Spice, Eminem or JAY-Z in inverted commas, though in the 1990s, 2000s and early 2010s respectively they might well have done. (JAY-Z is perhaps a bad example, because he used to put a diaeresis – two dots, see page 159 – over the y, has changed his mind more than once on the subject of the hyphen, and as of 2017 has decided to write his name in all capitals. Who knows, by the time this book is published he may be calling himself *'J-Zee'* in inverted commas. He seems to be running the punctuational gamut from J to Z.)

Headline writers use this sort of quotation mark for unconfirmed reports: a headline might read *'Corruption rife in local government'*, while the article goes on to explain that a disgruntled former employee has made this unsubstantiated accusation. The quotation marks thus become shorthand for the word *allegedly*.

A review of Brett Kahr's *Coffee with Freud* referred to *posthumous 'interviews' with Sigmund Freud*. Those quotes tell us that the supposed interviews in the book are the product of the author's imagination – he isn't claiming to be speaking to Freud via a ouija board.

A caption in an art exhibition I visited told me that a certain artist's technique *gave him an opportunity to work on a more intimate, 'artistic' level than his commercial output allowed*. Those distance quotes suggest that the caption-writer isn't convinced and that the sentence could be paraphrased – perhaps a little tactlessly – to give *what he liked to think of as a more intimate, artistic level*. You could introduce a similar note of sarcasm by writing, say, *the so-called 'aristocracy'*, suggesting that if you had your way they would all be piled into a tumbril and hauled off to the guillotine.

Recently we have also seen distance quotes with reference to social media, where old words have taken on a new and specific meaning: *she 'friended' me on*

Facebook; the restaurant I reviewed 'liked' my tweet. The use of quotes in this context tells you something about the writer: it looks as if she is new to social media and a bit uncomfortable with the jargon. A habitual user, accustomed to the media's vocabulary, wouldn't feel the need to put them in.

One word of warning about distance quotes: like making those little signs with your fingers, they become annoying if used too often.

Just what do you mean by that?

Quotation marks can be used to indicate that one party to a conversation is querying what the other has just said:

> *'Our children are grown up, so we're less at risk.'*
> *'"At risk"?'*
> *'Well, they're not going to be kidnapped on the way home from school.'*

If you (the second speaker) were saying this out loud, you'd convey the question by the intonation of your voice; on paper, the quotation marks do the job for you.

And take a moment to digest the punctuation of that question. It's a bit like the 'How are you?' 'Really busy' example I gave earlier. If it looks odd, expand it: if you wrote *'What do you mean, "at risk"?'* (which is, after all, what the speaker means), it would be clear that *at risk* was not in itself a question – it was an echoing of the first speaker's words.

→

So the double quotation marks come *before* the question mark, which in turn comes before the single quotation mark, which indicates the end of what the second speaker has said.

Exhausted? Take a breath and go on to the next chapter. It'll let you off the hook.

~

9

Things That Don't Matter Any More

This may be a slightly contentious heading. Perhaps I should have called it 'Things that are on the way out' or 'Things that don't matter – much – as long as you're consistent'.

Anyway.

From our own correspondent

Back in the day, if you happened to go to secretarial college or take a typing course at school, you would have been taught how to lay out letters – for the simple reason that once you went to work you would spend most of your time typing them. One of the rules was that, after the 'salutation'

- *Dear Whoever You Are* - you put a comma; after the signing-off formula - *Yours sincerely, Yours faithfully,* etc. - you put another. This is no longer the norm: neither my bank nor the National Health Service, both of whom have written to me recently, do it, and many more or less formal letters end with 'Kind regards' or even 'Best wishes', with or without a comma.

It's not that it's wrong to use the commas; it's perhaps that the casual way we begin and end emails has infiltrated formal correspondence. The only rule now is - as so often - be consistent. If you put a comma after the salutation, put one after your sign-off, too.

Secretarial college also taught you to put two spaces after a full stop: it was said to improve readability in an earlier generation of typesetting. It's completely unnecessary in today's world; if you are typing something for publication, most publishers will ask you to stick to one space and will remove the second one if you put it in.

Abbrevs. and contractions

We're under the heading 'strictly speaking' here. Or possibly 'life's too short'. With that proviso, an abbreviation is a word or words with the end(s) chopped off - *BBC, NASA, Co* (for *company*), *p* (for *page*). A contraction has the middle left out: *Mr, Dr, Ltd, nr* (for *near*). British English has traditionally followed the rule that an abbreviation is followed by a full stop (*B.B.C., Co.*) but that a contraction is not. It's a comparatively recent tradition: Jane Austen meticulously used a full stop in the names of Mr. and Mrs. Bennet, Mr. Darcy and Mr. Bingley. Dickens did the same with Mr. Bumble and Mr. Micawber. Most British writers would now say that this was dated and would use a full stop only to avoid ambiguity: to distinguish no. (short for the French *numéro*, meaning number) from the negative *no*, for example, or *a.m.* (*ante meridiem* – before midday) from *am*, a form of the verb *to be*. And, to continue to harp about consistency, if you use *a.m.* for *ante meridiem*, you should use *p.m.* for *post meridiem* – after midday – even though *pm* in itself and in lower case is unlikely to be ambiguous. Some people put AM and PM in small capitals, which is fine with me; PM in capitals, however, generally means *Prime Minister* (or, in specialist settings, *post-mortem*) and you wouldn't want to get into a muddle about those. Particularly if you were a pathologist.

James Joyce slips up

In a rare moment of reader-friendliness in *Ulysses* (see page 18), Joyce – yes, him again – refers to a printed pricelist in a café: *in unmistakable figures, coffee 2d., confectionery do., and honestly well worth twice the money once in a way*. The full stop after *2d* indicates that it is short for *denarius*, the old word for penny, while after *do* it shows that the word is not *do* but *ditto*, meaning 'the same' – so confectionery was also priced

$\longrightarrow$

at tuppence. Two meticulous pieces of punctuation in a single sentence, in a book renowned for the opposite. Perhaps that's what Joyce meant by *unmistakable figures*.

The common Latin abbreviations *i.e.* (*that is*), *e.g.* (*for example*) and *etc.* (*and so on*) are also often written with full stops, perhaps because *ie* and *eg* in particular look odd without them, perhaps because those who persist in using Latin abbreviations tend to be purists. There's a school of thought that says we should do away with these altogether, but as long as we carry on using them, we may as well use them lucidly.

A number of words in common use today are abbreviations of longer words: most people would recognize that *exam* is short for *examination* and *phone* for *telephone*, but may have forgotten that *bus* comes from *omnibus* (a Latin word meaning 'for everybody'), *cello* from *violoncello* and *flu* from *influenza*. There was a time when these shortened forms would have been written with an apostrophe before them or a full stop afterwards: *exam.*, *'phone*, *'bus*, *'cello* and even, purest of the pure, *'flu.* or *'flu'*. Not to mention *bra.*, *hippo.*, *rhino.*, *gym.* and *deli.* I've seen *exam.* and *'bus* in writings as late as the 1940s, but all of these words are now considered *clipped forms* rather than abbreviations. There are some clipped forms – *doc* for *doctor*, *gator* for *alligator*, *sec* for *second*, *mo* for *moment* – that are still regarded as too casual for formal writing, but whatever the context they are treated as words in their own right and don't need the punctuation.

What this boils down to is that, in the course of about the last hundred years, writing, say, *'phone* or *'bus* has gone from being correct to being old-fashioned, then pretentious and finally just plain weird. Be careful where you say that, though: a few years ago I was in Cambridge and there were building works in what I thought was called Benet Street. But no. Not only the permanent street signs but also the temporary hoarding on the scaffolding that assured me shops were open as usual spelled it Bene't. There's also a church called St Bene't's, apparently the oldest building in Cambridge. 'Nothing odd about it,' said my local friend, when I remarked on this odd use of an apostrophe. 'It's short for Benedict.' Like the users of Latin abbreviations, sign-writers in centres of academe appear to be purists.

10

Things That Have Their Uses

Diacritic marks

Many European languages make frequent and practical use of diacritic marks. That term embraces accents such as the French acute, grave and circumflex (as in *santé*, *très* and *château* respectively), the Spanish tilde (*ñ*), the German umlaut (*ü*) and various others, most of which indicate how the letter is to be pronounced or how the word is to be stressed. The tilde, for example, produces a sound like the one Brits (though not Americans) use at the beginning of *new* or *numerical* rather than *nail* or *normal* and indicates that *mañana* doesn't really rhyme with *banana*. The French cedilla (*ç*) tells us that *façade* and *garçon* have an *s* rather than a *k* sound in the middle, while the umlaut helps us to pronounce *über* with a long *oo* sound, more like *super* than *rubber*.

In Italian and Spanish, most words are stressed on the second-last syllable: an accent tells us when this is not the case, as in the Italian *caffè* and *qualità* and the Spanish *vámonos* and *clásico*. It also helps to distinguish between, say, *ancora*, meaning *still* or *yet*, and *àncora*, meaning *anchor*.

English, for once plumping for simplicity, scarcely bothers with any of this. We'll hang on to the accents when we're using a word or expression of obviously foreign extraction – *à la carte, blasé, coup de grâce, doppelgänger* – and especially when an accent on a final e indicates that it is to be pronounced: *outré, passé* or a newspaper's *exposé* of a scandal, which would otherwise look just like the familiar English verb *to expose*. We'll also use them (as a basic courtesy) in order to spell someone's name correctly: *Niccolò Machiavelli, Gérard Depardieu, Raúl*.

It's easy to become precious about this, though: if a word has become so familiar as hardly to be foreign any more, it's time to drop the accent(s). If you were writing about the French film genre *cinéma-vérité*, for example, the accents would be appropriate; to put one on *cinéma* when you just mean you are going to see a movie would be downright pseud. I'd feel the same about *gâteau*: fine, keep the accent if you are referring to something specific such as a Gâteau St Honoré (and if you don't know what that is, Google it – it's quite spectacular), but leave it off if you're talking about any old creamy cake. Particularly one that claims to originate in the (German) Black Forest.

Very occasionally in English we use a *diaeresis* – typographically the same thing as the German *umlaut* – over the second of two vowels to show that they are to be pronounced separately. *Naïve* and the girl's name *Zoë* are two examples (those two little dots warn us that the words don't rhyme with *waive* and *toe*). But both of these are becoming less common – as indeed is the acknowledgement that, in the original French, *naïve* is a feminine form; you might describe an artistic style as *naïf*, but it would be old-fashioned to the point of pedantry to write about a *naïf* young man, with or without the diaeresis.

¿How did you know what I was going to say?

Spanish has an interesting trick that I've often felt would come in handy in other languages. At the start of a question or an exclamation, it puts an upside-down version of the relevant punctuation mark: ¿ or ¡. It might not seem necessary in something short like *Who's there?* or *Help me!*, and even in longer constructions English tends to use obvious question-words such as *where* or *what*, or to help us out with word order (*Didn't I tell you that I was going to be late?*), so that we know from the start that we are dealing with a question. But how about something like *If I had known he had such disgusting manners, I should never have asked him to stay!* An inverted exclamation mark at the start would help us put the right level of indignation into our tone as we read it. Just a thought.

As a footnote ...

There are a few other marks that deserve a mention, because you will sometimes see them in print and might find them useful yourself.

The *caret mark* (^) indicates that something has been left out and should be re-instated: you'd most often see it handwritten in the margin of a typeset text. The name is Latin for 'it is lacking'.

The *asterisk* (*) and the *obelisk, obelus* or (commonly) *dagger* (†) are usually used to indicate a footnote or endnote. In some texts, notes are numbered, but where there are no more than one or two on a page, these symbols are often preferred. They can even be doubled up (** and ‡) if more notes are needed. Asterisks can also indicate that you don't want to spell out a swear word, even though your readers are unlikely to think that *s**t* means *suit, sort* or *salt*.

Asterisk means a star and *obelisk* comes from a word meaning spit – in the sense of a sticking-out piece of land, rather than what you do after you've rinsed your mouth out. Note that both these words end in *-sk*, so are pronounced like *risk* and *task*; if you pronounce them *asteriks* and *obeliks*, as many people do, you are confusing them with the famous cartoon Gauls.

I'm including the *pilcrow* (¶), once used to mark the start of a paragraph, because I like the name; it sounds as if it's been made up as an anagram of something else – *crow lip*, perhaps, or *clip row*. In fact, its origins seem to be connected – sensibly enough, given its purpose – with *paragraph*. Google 'pilcrow in manuscript' and you'll find images of centuries-old text with this symbol, often ornately drawn in red or blue ink, sometimes appearing in the middle of lines. When the invention of the printing press hurried up production, ornamentation became time-consuming and instead of the pretty marks we ended up with white spaces. The price of progress, eh?

The solidus (/), also known as an *oblique*, *virgule*, *forward slash* or – and this will really wow the next stranger you buttonhole at a party – *separatrix*, has a multitude of uses, historical and current. In old (British and Commonwealth) money, it was used to separate pounds, shilling and pence: thus £5/3/6 meant five pounds, three shillings and sixpence, while 8/4 meant eight shillings and fourpence. It marks the line breaks if you are writing verse without setting it in lines: *The Owl and the Pussy-cat went to sea/In a beautiful pea-green boat*. It can also be used in a date to separate day from month from year (as in 4/11/17, meaning 4 November 2017 or 11 April 2017, depending on which continent you're on); in an address to separate a flat number from a building number (7/103 Maple Street); to divide the two parts of a fraction (1/2, 11/16); in expressions such as *and/ or*; in web addresses and in various other more obscure or specialist fields. The solidus's mirror image, the *backslash* (\), was introduced into early programming languages and is still used mostly in computing.

Odds and ends that might catch on

My favourite of these is the potentially useful device called an *interrobang*: a combination of a *question* (or *interrogation*) *mark* and an *exclamation mark*, which in old printing jargon was called a *bang*. Said to have been invented by an American editor called Martin Speckter in the 1960s, the interrobang has been described as the typographical equivalent of a grimace or a shrug of the shoulders. Speckter is quoted as saying that it was used exclusively for rhetorical questions along the lines of 'You call that a hat?!' More recently, it's been described as the punctuational equivalent of OMGWTF.

On a pre-computer typewriter you could produce an interrobang by typing a question mark, back-spacing and typing an exclamation mark over it. Most modern keyboards don't permit that, so we are stuck with typing the two characters separately – *?!* or, for real emphasis, *???!!!!* In fact, it seems wrong to have typed OMGWTF at the end of the last paragraph without the addition of at least one *?!*

Then there's the *percontation mark*, popular for a while in the sixteenth and seventeenth centuries. It was a mirror image of a question mark, placed, unlike the upside-down Spanish one, at the end of a question (below left). But the question had to be a rhetorical one, and the implication seems to have been that the percontation mark made the question sarcastic, so that the person being asked it looked stupid. A variation on this theme, known as the *irony mark*, was proposed by a French novelist called Hervé Bazin in the 1960s: the difference is that the irony mark comes at the beginning of the question, is smaller than a regular question mark and is raised a little above the baseline, like an opening inverted comma (below right).

Bazin was full of bright ideas about punctuation. He also suggested:

- the *acclamation point*, which looks a bit like two exclamation marks with the right-hand one tilted to the right (see next page): he described this as 'the stylistic representation of those two little flags that float above the tour bus when a president comes to town' and suggested it be used to show goodwill and welcome.

- the *certitude point (below)*, to be used when you want to stress how strongly you believe what you are saying; it's like a right-tilted exclamation mark with a line through it.

- the *authority point* (below), like a certitude point except that the line through it is curved; this, according to Bazin, 'shades your sentence' with authority, 'like a parasol over a sultan'.

He had others, including one specifically designed to enclose a loving message, but although they have inspired wide enthusiasm across the internet, they haven't made it big time into print. Maybe they are all too difficult to reproduce on most keyboards. Or, when you get down to thinking about them, not as useful as they seem at first glance. Sorry, Hervé, I admire your enthusiasm and love your imagery, but do we really need more punctuation marks that we don't quite understand how to use?

11

Things That Have No Rules

It's easy for purists, pundits and old fogies to say that the world in general and punctuation in particular are going to the dogs because of the way language has been adapted to suit text messaging and social media. But I think it's important to remember, before we get too up in arms, that this isn't bad English; it is *different* English. The distinguished American lexicographer John McWhorter has called it 'fingered speech' – talking that happens to be written down. If you were giving a lecture or accepting an award, you would probably prepare what you were going to say, think about your choice of words and try not to repeat yourself or to ramble on too long. But in casual conversation, you don't generally stop and consider every word before you utter it.

The same distinction applies with the written word. As with the lecture, you would take care over a formal report or a job application, give thought to capital letters and not splatter every sentence with multiple exclamation marks. But in today's world of instant communication, you let what you want to say pour out of you, and devil take the apostrophes.

Part of the reason for this is that text messages, tweets and the like are designed for speed; and another is that they are often typed on smartphones with keyboards too small to carry lots of characters at once. On my phone (and it's a famous brand, so I don't suppose I am alone in this), the only symbol available on the letters keyboard is a full stop, so even a comma requires a bit of effort, and I have to press a special key if I want to produce a capital letter. No wonder busy and/or impatient people don't bother with apostrophes and semicolons.

That said, there are times when that bit of effort might pay dividends, if we remember that punctuation is there to help clarify meaning. I have one friend who has embraced textspeak with the enthusiasm of someone who has young grandchildren. Reporting on recent visits to the cinema, she told me what she thought of *la la land*, with no capitalization. That was OK: at the time you would have had to live on another planet not to be aware of that film, and it's an unusual and recognizable name. I was a bit thrown, though, when she wrote, *off to see lion tomorrow*.

This brings me to points that I think are worth making about punctuation in these informal contexts:

- It's important to be able to distinguish between times when correct punctuation matters and when it doesn't. It's also good to be able to use it correctly when it does matter.

- Even when you're doing nothing more life-threatening than texting a friend about a movie, it's useful to be able to distinguish between a title and a wild beast.

Say it with ????

Punctuation's ability to convey emotion comes into its own when you want to be brief. If you receive a message you don't understand, replying with nothing more than *???* is a convenient way of saying 'Sorry, I have no idea what you mean', while *!!!!!* could mean 'Wow, that is incredible news; no, I hadn't heard'. The number of question or exclamation marks is entirely up to you and dependent on the amount of confusion or emotion you want to express.

Then there is the whole range of dingbats, emoticons and the more sophisticated emojis. Way back in 2013 – a lifetime ago in the development of modern communication – the news website *Business Insider* published an interview with an eighteen-year-old who said that she and her friends communicated almost exclusively with emojis. She reserved email, obviously a pretty passé concept as far as she was concerned, for schoolwork and admitted to phoning (and actually talking to) her parents, but 'no one else, really'.

And you can see why. Those cunning little devices allow you to convey anything from tears of joy to deep-seated misery or uncontrollable rage, with more temperate variations to show that you are mildly upset or just a bit cross. You can give a suggestion a thumbs-up or -down, indicate that you are crossing your fingers or praying, or enliven your messages with flowers, hearts, frogs or slices of pizza. And you can adapt the many, many images available to suit your own needs: one young friend, expressing the wish that his correspondent would enjoy what was obviously going to be a tedious evening, ended his message with a pig and an aeroplane – the nearest he could get to 'Pigs might fly'.

Emotion in an icon

Here's a sidebar for trivia/word buffs. *Emoticon* is what is called a *portmanteau word*, where parts or the whole of two words are run together to produce something that includes the meaning of both. Thus *emoticon* is a combination of *emotion* and *icon* and means, of course, an icon that expresses feelings. *Emoji*, despite appearances, has nothing to do with emotion. If you were to break it into its component parts it would be *e-moji*, from the Japanese for *picture character*. Its resemblance to *emoticon* is one of those joyous little coincidences that make life worth living.

Despite my cinema-going granny friend – and an increasing number of people over the age of thirty who know the difference between a 🙂, a 😀 and a 😳 – there is still a bit of a generation-gap thing going on here. But remember what I was saying about Gutenberg and hot-metal type in the introduction? Well, dingbats, emoticons and emojis represent the first massive change in punctuation that has happened in over 500 years. Despite what I said a moment ago about having to change the keyboards to type a comma, the advent of the word-processor, the home computer, the tablet and the mobile phone has brought a whole new range of characters to our fingertips, changing the way we communicate beyond recognition, in the space of a single generation. No wonder some of us are a bit flummoxed.

But surely there is room for looking on a bright side. Bear in mind that today's younger generation has made a global superstar out of a singer whose first three albums were called +, × and ÷. Ed Sheeran fans presumably see nothing odd in this, even if their parents are wondering (if they happen to know the expression), 'WTF?' What these innovations are doing is bringing back those touches of personal taste and whimsy in which the medieval monks indulged. Emoji enthusiast Fred Benenson has 'translated' all of *Moby Dick* into emojis. Not only that, but he has published it and archived it in the Library of Congress, where it sits alongside every other book published in the United States – most of them in more conventional form. And why has he done this? Because he can. Is it any dafter than climbing Mount Everest 'because it was there'? I don't think so. It's certainly a lot less dangerous. I'm inclined to celebrate this sort of creativity – perhaps with a slice of pizza 🍕.

~

References

The following were all very useful to me as I was researching this book. I particularly recommend the works of the great David Crystal for anyone wanting erudite but highly readable guides to many aspects of language.

Crystal, David, *Making a Point: The Pernickety Story of English Punctuation* (Profile, 2015)

Fowler, H. W., *A Dictionary of Modern English Usage* (Oxford, 1926)

Matchett, Carol, *Key Stage 2 Punctuation* (Schofield & Sims, 2015)

Spelling, Punctuation and Grammar for GCSE (CGP Books, 2015)

Trask, R. L., *Penguin Guide to Punctuation* (Penguin, 1997)

For information on the origins of punctuation:
http://www.bbc.com/culture/story/20150902-the-mysterious-origins-of-punctuation

On emojis:
http://www.businessinsider.com/how-teens-use-emojis-to-talk-2013-10?IR=T

On the percontation point:
http://mentalfloss.com/article/12710/13-little-known-punctuation-marks-we-should-be-using

In addition, I have used the following to give examples of different styles in punctuation:

Adichie, Chimamanda Ngozi, *The Thing Around Your Neck* (4th Estate, 2009)

Armitage, Simon, *Walking Home* (Faber, 2012)

Bail, Murray, *The Voyage* (Text Publishing, 2012)

Betjeman, John, *Coming Home: An Anthology of Prose* (Methuen, 1997)

Boyd, William, *Any Human Heart* (Hamish Hamilton, 2002)

Bryson, Bill, *At Home* (Doubleday, 2010)

Carrión, Jorge, *Bookshops* (translated by Peter Bush, MacLehose Press, 2016)

Christie, Agatha, *Mrs McGinty's Dead* (Collins, 1952)

Dallek, Robert, *John F. Kennedy: An Unfinished Life* (Penguin, 2004)

Dickens, Charles, *Great Expectations* (Book-of-the-Month Club 1997; first published 1861)

Farrell, J. G., *Troubles* (Jonathan Cape, 1970)

Fforde, Katie, *Artistic Licence* (Century, 2001)

Frayn, Michael, *The Russian Interpreter* (1966, reissued by Faber & Faber, 2015)

Golding, William, *Lord of the Flies* (Faber, 1954)

Gregory, Philippa, *The Other Queen* (HarperCollins, 2008)

Heyer, Georgette, *The Grand Sophy* (Heinemann, 1950)

Heyer, Georgette, *A Christmas Party* (originally published as *Envious Casca*, 1941, reissued by Arrow Books, 2015)

Hill, Reginald, *The Death of Dalziel* (HarperCollins, 2007)

Jackman, Brian, *Wild About Britain* (Bradt, 2017)

Joyce, James, *Ulysses* (Penguin, 1992; first published 1922)

Kelman, James, *How Late It Was, How Late* (Secker, 1994)

Lawrence, D. H., *Lady Chatterley's Lover* (Penguin, 1960)

Leon, Donna, *Drawing Conclusions* (Heinemann, 2011)

Manners, Jamie, *The Seven Noses of Soho* (Michael O'Mara, 2015)

May, Peter, *The Blackhouse* (Quercus, 2011)

Selby Jr, Hubert, *Last Exit to Brooklyn* (Penguin, 2011; first published 1964)

Self, Will, *Shark* (Viking, 2014)

Sellar, W. C. and Yeatman, R. J., *1066 and All That* (Methuen, 1930)

Spufford, Francis, *Golden Hill* (Faber, 2016)

Stein, Gertrude, *The Autobiography of Alice B. Toklas* (Penguin, 2001; first published 1933)

The Collected Novellas of Stefan Zweig (translated by Anthea Bell, Pushkin Press, 2015)

Acknowledgements

Most of my books have been greatly helped by the contributions of eagle-eyed, witty and/or pedantic friends and relations, and *Help a Thief!* is no exception. My thanks this time to Ann, the two Carols and Cec, for sharing examples of infelicitous punctuation, and to Niki and Callum for updating the thought that pigs might fly.

Thanks also to Louise, George, Emily and everyone else at Michael O'Mara Books for their enthusiasm and attention to detail, and for producing such a fine-looking book.

Index

N

O

P

About the Author

Caroline Taggart worked in publishing as an editor of popular non-fiction for thirty years before being asked by Michael O'Mara Books to write *I Used to Know That*, which became a *Sunday Times* bestseller. Following that she was co-author of *My Grammar and I (or should that be 'Me'?)*, and has since written a number of other books about words and English usage including nine titles for Michael O'Mara Books. Caroline has appeared frequently on television and on national and regional radio, talking about language, grammar and whether or not Druids Cross should have an apostrophe.

Her website is carolinetaggart.co.uk and you can follow her on Twitter @citaggart.

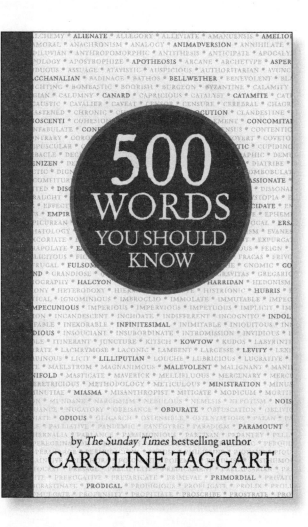

500 Words You Should Know

978-1-78243-294-4

£9.99

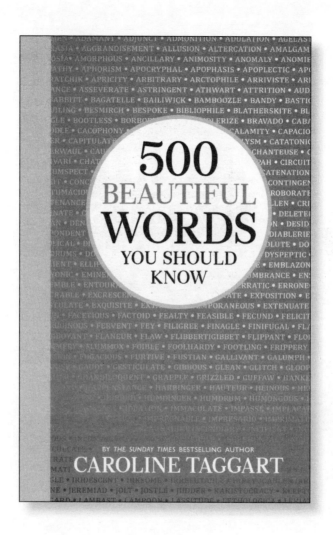

500 Beautiful Words You Should Know
978-1-78929-227-5
£9.99

New Words for Old

978-1-78243-472-6

£9.99